DIRECT ACTION & SABOTAGE

Three Classic IWW Pamphlets from the 1910s

DIRECT ACTION & SABOTAGE

Three Classic IWW Pamphlets from the 1910s

Elizabeth Gurley Flynn
Walker C. Smith
William E. Trautmann

Edited & Introduced by
Salvatore Salerno

Charles H. Kerr Library   PM Press

A NOTE ON THE ILLUSTRATIONS
All the illustrations in this book appeared originally in the *Industrial Worker*
or other official IWW publications. However, only those on the covers of the
three pamphlets reprinted here actually appeared in those pamphlets.

Direct Action & Sabotage: Three Classic IWW Pamphlets from the 1910s
Elizabeth Gurley Flynn, Walker C. Smith, and William E. Trautmann
Edited by Salvatore Salerno

© PM Press 2014

PM Press
PO Box 23912
Oakland, CA 94623
www.pmpress.org

Published in conjunction with the Charles H. Kerr Publishing Company
C.H. Kerr Company
1726 Jarvis Avenue
Chicago, IL 60626
www.charleshkerr.com

Cover design by Josh MacPhee
Layout by Jonathan Rowland

ISBN: 978-1-60486-482-3
Library of Congress Control Number: 2013911525

10 9 8 7 6 5 4 3 2

Printed in the USA

CONTENTS

The Cat Comes Back – Legally

The IWW welcomed the Wildcat Strikes and
Sitdowns of the 1930s as the offspring of the Wobbly
Black Cat of Direct Action and Sabotage.

Direct Action & Sabotage!

Is the machine more than its makers?
Sabotage says "No!"

Is the product greater than producers?
Sabotage says "No!"

Sabotage places human life—
and especially the life of the only useful class—
higher than all else in the universe.

For sabotage or for slavery?
Which?

—Walker C. Smith

The Rebel's Toast

If Freedom's road seems rough and hard,
And strewn with rocks and thorns,
Then put your wooden shoes on, pard,
And you won't hurt your corns.
To organize and teach, no doubt,
Is very good, that's true,
But still we can't succeed without
The Good Old Wooden Shoe.

—Joe Hill

MR. BLOCK

HE DON'T FAVOR SABOTAGE

Cartoon by Ernest Riebe

Introduction

The Industrial Workers of the World (IWW), founded in 1905, distinguished itself from other revolutionary workers' organizations by its emphasis on working-class solidarity and classwide collective action as the means of social transformation. The IWW was not, strictly speaking, pacifist in outlook, but its spokespersons and literature consistently opposed those Marxists and anarchists who proposed armed struggle, seizure of state power, or other forms of organized or individual violence as the road to revolution in the U.S. Historian Staughton Lynd was thus fully justified in featuring the IWW prominently in his anthology on *Nonviolence in America.*[1]

As the pamphlets reproduced in this volume attest, the IWW notions of direct action and sabotage are also firmly within the framework of nonviolence, for they have absolutely nothing to do with any form of life-threatening "terrorism" or personal injury.

The pamphlets reprinted here were first published in the 1910s, amidst great controversy and division within the left regarding the value of these tactics. Even then, the tactics of direct action and sabotage were often associated with the cartoonists' image of the disheveled, wild-eyed anarchist armed with stiletto, handgun or bomb—the clandestine activity of a militant minority or the desperate acts of the unorganized. The mainstream, trade-union and left press of the period all shared in creating and perpetuating this false and stereotyped image which associated the wanton destruction of property and human life with the practices of sabotage and direct action. The activist authors of the texts in this collection challenged the prevailing stereotype and redefined the parameters of the debate. As they point out, the *practice* of direct action, and of sabotage, are as old as class society itself, and have been an integral part of the everyday work life of wage-earners in all times and places. To the IWW belongs the distinction of being the first workers' organization in the U.S. to discuss these common practices openly, and to recognize their place in working-class struggle. Viewing direct action and sabotage in the spirit of creative nonviolence, Wobblies readily integrated these tactics into their struggle to build industrial unions.

Notes on the History of Direct Action and Sabotage

All who have written on the subject of direct action and sabotage remind us of the ancient origins of these tactics. Pamphleteers and soapboxers who advocated such resistance, in their street corner speeches and writings, claimed that direct action and sabotage were as old as exploitation and had long been part of labor's arsenal. As forms of resistance and struggle, direct action and sabotage emerged in opposition to the myriad social injustices of civil society, imperialist conquest and industrial development. Direct action and sabotage range from individual acts of rebellion and resistance or action on the part of small groups, to larger patterns of action within the context of a culture of struggle. As forms of struggle and resistance they were often hidden and anonymous, their origin and history shrouded by mystery, preserved in oral tradition and iconography, named or made visible after the fact. The history of these tactics often reveals a tension between nonviolent direct action and quasi-insurrectionary activity, a tension that continues to be debated among activists today.

The earliest recorded forms of direct action and sabotage emerge in antiquity. In Aristophanes' *Lysistrata*, women attacked the economic heart of the ancient household and the roots of militarism; slaves and gladiators of Rome carried out revolts against the authority of the polis; builders of the Temple and Palace went on strike in Jerusalem in 29 B.C. and the Greek silver miners rebelled at Laurium in 413 B.C.[2] These examples establish the ancient ancestry of direct action. Other early examples include social banditry, peasant uprisings and the struggle of Africans against new world slavery. Enslaved Africans carried out revolts at the point of embarkation, during the middle passage, and at the shore "warehouse." In the United States they created an illegal, grapevine system of communication capable, it was said, of "running several hundred miles in a fortnight." The underground served insurrectionary activity and aided runaways. On the plantation enslaved Africans fought to set their own tempo and rhythm of work. Frederick Douglass writes:

> There is much rivalry among slaves, at times, as to which can do the most work, and masters generally seek to promote such rivalry. But some of them were too wise to race with each other very long. Such racing, we had the sagacity to see, was not likely to pay. We had our times for measuring each other's strength, but we knew too much to keep up the competition so long as to produce an extraordinary days work. We knew that if, by extraordinary exertion, a large quantity of work was done in one day, the fact, becoming known to the master, might lead him to require the same amount every day. This thought was enough to bring us to a dead halt when ever so much excited for the race.

Little is known about black workplace sabotage, and even less about its relationship to working-class resistance. Robin D.G. Kelley writes in *Race Rebels*:

Judging from existing histories, it seems domestic workers adopted sabotage techniques more frequently than industrial workers. There is ample evidence of household workers scorching or spitting in food, damaging kitchen appliances and breaking appliances, but these acts were generally dismissed by employers and white contemporaries as proof of black moral and intellectual inferiority.[3]

Peasants struggling against landlords and other minions of the state burned property deeds and debt notes, and expropriated tax holdings.[4] In industrializing cities throughout Europe increases in bread prices, the introduction of new machinery and enclosures were met with resistance. Sustained illegal action or quasi-insurrectionary activity such as Luddism also emerged. Some forms of quasi-insurrectionary activity were deliberate, others spontaneous. E.P. Thompson writes that spontaneous direct action rooted in local working-class culture was

> rarely a mere uproar which culminated in the breaking open of barns or the looting of shops. It was legitimised by the assumption of the older moral economy, which taught the immorality of any unfair method of forcing up the price of provisions by profiteering upon the necessities of the people.

Direct action rooted in working-class culture affirmed basic human values, empowering individuals to act collectively in behalf of the community.[5]

Emergence of These Tactics within the Labor Movement

In *The Condition of the Working Class* Engels initiated a critique of direct action which came to define the policy of the

First International. Workers' struggle, Engels wrote, had passed "'through several phases': theft and crime, machine-breaking, trade union organization and strikes, the struggle for state power."[6] These tactics, he concluded—with the exception, in certain instances, of the strike—proved a hindrance to the workers' larger political struggle for conquest of state power. Viewed against the larger objective of abolishing bourgeois domination and wage labor, such methods had proved to be at best impediments, and in many instances self-defeating. Sabotage and direct action, Engels argued, were primitive and crude methods belonging to a past era; it was time they were replaced by better ones.

The International Working Men's Association or First International affirmed the primacy of political struggle, condemning actions which would hinder parliamentary objectives. These positions were confronted by the Anti-Authoritarians at the First International's congress at Basel (1869). This coalition of anarchists, militant trade unionists and social revolutionaries called for the abandonment of political action, challenging the International's founding principles. In his report to the congress, Eugene Hins introduced into discussion the idea of workers' councils as the instrument of class struggle and the structural basis of the coming libertarian society. The new society would be administered from the point of production by workers, ending forever the old system of government based on injustice and greed. These ideas, derived from the writings and activities of Mikhail Bakunin and other anarchists, had gained support in sections of the International in Belgium, Holland, the Swiss Jura, France and Spain. Following the London Conference of the International in 1871, these sections formed the Anti-Authoritarian International in response to the attempt by Marx and Engels to centralize the powers of the International's General Council.[7]

In the 1870s numerous Anti-Authoritarian sections of the International appeared in New York, Boston and other American cities. *The Word*, a libertarian monthly magazine founded by Ezra Haywood in Princeton, Massachusetts, began publishing

Bakunin's writings. *Woodhull and Claflin's Weekly* and *The Word* became the unofficial organs of the Anti-Authoritarians.[8] These journals defended the principles of decentralist socialism and criticized the authoritarian orientation of the General Council. In the U.S. there were also a number of adherents of the Bakuninist wing of the International among foreign-language groups. Principally refugees from the Paris Commune, these immigrants established sections in New York and New Jersey and sent delegates to the Anti-Authoritarian International that met in St. Imier, Switzerland in 1872.[9]

The movement for decentralist socialism and militant trade unionism became worldwide during the 1880s and '90s. Developing out of indigenous strike culture, the movement grew through intricate patterns of "cross fertilization" between countries and continents. Though the early movement was a mixture of philosophies and theories derived from socialism and anarchism, it did not represent a closed system of ideas, but rather paralleled developments in workers' struggles against technological development and economic conditions. Increasingly international in influence, the movement sought to create a more revolutionary basis for trade union struggles.[10]

In France this tendency coincided with widespread disillusionment with the *attentats* of the militant anarchist and social revolutionaries. In the 1890s, many anarchists entered the trade union movement while others emigrated to escape police repression and continue their activity. Anarchists such as Ferdinand Pelloutier and Emile Pouget had a great impact on the international trade union movement. Through their efforts, the idea that a confederation of labor unions could manage the economy in a stateless society gave birth to the Confederation Generale du Travail (General Confederation of Labor) in 1895. Following the C.G.T.'s founding convention, French syndicalists began speaking about the "direct initiative" of the worker and of "unional activity imposing 'directly' a reform upon the employer" in their discussion about tactics and methods. In 1897 Ferdinand Pelloutier coined the term "direct action" to describe the overall practice emerging from the revolutionary syndicalist movement.[11]

Just as the practice of direct action existed long before it was named or had become part of a specific movement or trade union strategy, the same is also true of sabotage. Some authors date the origins of the term to the French silkweavers' strike in Lyons in 1834.[12] In this strike, silkweavers used their sabots (wooden shoes) to smash both glass and machinery. This explanation connects the origins of the term to the earlier practices of the Luddites in Britain. In other versions of the term's origins, the practice is connected to a French worker who threw his sabot to disable but not wreck machinery. In perhaps the most plausible explanation for the term's origins, Franklin Rosemont argues that the term entered French artisan usage "to describe the clumsiness of scabs brought in from rural areas where wooden shoes continued to be worn after they had passed out of use in the city."[13] Sabotage therefore came to denote the clumsy work of the sabot-clad scab as an alternative to the walkout. This explanation is consistent with Emile Pouget, the French anarcho-syndicalist, who describes "sabotage" as a slang expression meaning "to work clumsily as if by sabot blows." Though adopted by the C.G.T.'s Congress of Toulouse in 1897, Pouget points out that sabotage did not have a Parisian trademark. Citing the activities of Glasgow dockworkers in an 1889 strike, Pouget argued that, if anything, it was a practice imported from across the channel and derived from a Scottish expression, "Go cannie" (Ca'canny) which means "go slow."[14]

In the U.S., similar ideas were beginning to take root among labor activists. The German anarchist Johann Most played a decisive role among immigrant revolutionaries. Reaching the U.S. in 1882, he became involved in the social revolutionary movement. Most helped draft the "Pittsburgh Manifesto" which established the International Working People's Association (the so-called Black International), and galvanized the social revolutionary movement. Most and his followers objected to any form of compromise with existing institutions and declared their opposition to trade unions and their struggle for immediate economic gain. The Pittsburgh Manifesto also rejected all political parties—thereby denying the Marxists' belief in the necessity of a revolutionary party of the proletariat—and called for direct action on the industrial field.

In the late 1890s when the syndicalist movement in France attracted worldwide attention following the conferences at Limoges (1895) and Tours (1896), Most made himself spokesperson of the new movement in the U.S. Through the *Freiheit* (Freedom), which he edited for twenty-seven years, Most introduced German and Russian immigrants in the needle, brewery and building trades to the movement's ideas and tactics. Seeing in European syndicalism "the practical form of organization for the realization of communist-anarchism," Most published all of the leaflet literature available at the time. In the *Freiheit* appeared the writings of Pelloutier, Pouget, Pierrot, John Turner, S. Nacht (Arnold Roller), Victor Dave, and other key propagandists for the syndicalist movement.[15]

Italian immigrants, working in mining, on track gangs or as factory workers, were also significant carriers of syndicalist politics and culture. In *Industrial Unionism: New Methods and New Forms*, William E. Trautmann uses the example of Italian construction workers in his discussion of direct action. When workers could not overcome police, injunction judges or jailors, Trautmann recommended following their example of striking on the job:

> In Harvey, Illinois, where contractors of railway construction work announced a reduction of 50 cents per day for the Italian workers, the latter, having learned enough of the principles of industrial unionism, decided at once to cut their shovels half an inch, and work with these cut shovels, which they did; and, with the protestation, "Short pay, short shovels," they forced the contractors to restore the former wages.

In Paterson, New Jersey, Italian and Spanish anarchists agitated for a workers' union based on anarcho-syndicalism. The group, calling itself "Right to Existence," organized in the silk industry and supported striking miners in Colorado. They formed the "Universita Populare" which organized public lectures, discussions, social gatherings and study groups. Many articles appeared in the pages of its newspaper, *La Questione Social,* reporting on the European revolutionary syndicalist movement as well as appealing to workers to adopt syndicalist tactics in their struggles against manufacturing magnates.[16]

Among the left or direct-actionist wing of the Socialist Party were many revolutionary socialists who leaned toward an anarcho-syndicalist version of industrial unionism. Chief among them was William E. Trautmann. His early pamphlet on direct action and sabotage was followed by those written by Walker C. Smith and Elizabeth Gurley Flynn. The three pamphlets collected in this volume represent the classic statements on worker militancy written by labor activists in the U.S. in the early 1910s.

William E. Trautmann: The Power of Folded Arms

An active pamphleteer, journalist and militant trade unionist, Trautmann's early writings on direct action and sabotage reflect his contact with the European syndicalist movement, his experiences on the shop floor and in the labor movement. Born in New Zealand to German parents, Trautmann was active in the socialist and labor movement in Germany and Russia before immigrating to the U.S. late in 1890. Settling in Ohio he became an organizer for the Brewery Workers Union (B.W.U.). Eventually he was elected to the union's General Executive Board and became editor of the union's rank and file paper *Brauer Zeitung* (Brewers' Journal).[17]

Between 1900 and 1905 Trautmann formulated many of the basic ideas which later represented the political and economic philosophy of the IWW. He is credited with being among the first to introduce American workers to a version of revolutionary industrial unionism which incorporated aspects of European syndicalism.[18] Writing in the special Labor Day issue of the *American Labor Union Journal* of 1903, Trautmann discussed his developing ideas of industrial unionism:

> Socialists abroad, as well as here, perceive that the instruments for the management of the socialist republic, now in process of formation, must be created, and they build the labor organizations according to this need. Who can judge how to regulate the required production of utilities in the various lines of industry better than those directly employed in a given industry? Industrial organizations are the forerunners of the society established on Socialist foundations.

During 1903 and 1904, Trautmann wrote various articles for the *Brauer Zeitung* reporting on issues galvanizing the European syndicalist movement. His articles and editorials discussed the inadequacy of the ballot, the general strike as a weapon in the class war, and syndicates as the basis for governing the future socialist society. Trautmann argued the power of the union movement did not lie in its ability to shape electoral constituencies, but in the union's potential to build active economic structures that would administer the new socialist society. The union, not the party, was the vehicle of revolutionary change; the general strike, not the ballot, would be the means of proletarian emancipation. Because of his intense activity with the nascent revolutionary industrial union movement, the General Executive Board of the B.W.U. removed Trautmann from his post as editor of the organization's journal early in 1905.[19]

At the IWW's founding convention Trautmann was elected general secretary-treasurer and member of the IWW's first General Executive Board. At the fourth convention in 1908,

Trautmann, Vincent St. John and other direct actionists eliminated the political clause in the IWW's preamble, ousted Daniel DeLeon, and turned the IWW toward organizational drives in the steel and textile mills of the East, lumber camps of the Northwest and Southwest, and farm lands of the Pacific Coast and Midwest. At this convention, Trautmann was replaced by St. John as secretary-treasurer and elected general organizer, a position he held until 1913. In 1909 he organized immigrant workers to win the first strike against the Steel Trust in McKees Rock, Pennsylvania. Between 1909 and 1912 he tried to establish IWW unions among rubber workers in Akron and automobile workers in Detroit and helped to direct the strike in Lawrence in 1912. Little is available on Trautmann's activity following the Lawrence strike.

Trautmann wrote *Direct Action and Sabotage* in 1912. It is among the earliest attempts at interpreting the principles and strategies of European syndicalism and applying them to the struggles of workers in the U.S. Though printed by the Socialist News Company, an IWW print shop, the pamphlet was not considered official literature. The IWW held that tactical success depended on the knowledge and initiative of the worker, not on its ability to advocate correct tactics. The IWW maintained that

> Direct action is not a cut and dried program which is used on every occasion regardless of the conditions which are to be contended with, but finds expression in the various phases as circumstances and the conditions of struggle may determine. Sabotage, though a new word, is as old as the labor movement. It is now assuming new and complex forms in relationship to that movement. We need not "advocate" it; we need only explain it. The organized worker will do the acting.[20]

The line between explanation and advocacy wore thin at times and became the subject of heated debate and factional disputes.

Written in the wake of the trial of the McNamaras, two activist brothers who were arrested for allegedly dynamiting the *Los Angeles Times* building (an explosion later attributed to a defective boiler),[21] *Direct Action and Sabotage* greeted a divided labor and political community. While the IWW had called for a general strike to protest their arrest, socialists and craft unionists made soapbox speeches denouncing direct action and sabotage as "terrorist" tactics aimed at the destruction of human life and property. The Socialist Party, objecting in general to the whole philosophy of direct action, became increasingly incensed by the syndicalist propaganda associated with the IWW, and moved at its 1912 convention to amend its constitution to exclude those who advocated sabotage. In February of 1913 the Socialist Party broke its tie with the IWW by expelling William D. Haywood from the party's National Executive Committee.[22]

In his pamphlet, Trautmann neither condemned violent methods of struggle nor unconditionally sanctioned their use. He argued that mass organizations in their applications of direct action could not always refrain from violent and destructive methods. Trautmann maintained that the standard for judging violent forms of sabotage and direct action was whether they achieved their result or ended in the subversion of their original aim. Forms of direct action and sabotage, whether violent or nonviolent, which did not "undermine the economic power of the employing class" while providing for the "social protection and advancement of the working class" were not direct action but constituted antisocial behavior.

Trautmann also turned his attention to the ways the capitalist used sabotage to defeat worker resistance, noting that the capitalist who was quickest to denounce violence was its greatest perpetrator.

> The strike, local, general or universal, is answered with the lockout locally, in industries, universally, if need be and when they are prepared for it. Irritation strikes

they meet with the closing down of their factories or mines in one district and overtaxed operations of their factories and workshops in other districts. Political action by the workers they answer with the withdrawal of the rights of free speech, free assemblage and coalition, and by the use of their servile tools. . . . They counteract the boycott with their blacklists . . .

The significance of Trautmann's pamphlet lies in his attention to the successes of French syndicalists in using nonviolent direct action to curtail the length of strikes and to strike on the job when the strike would only end in a lockout.[23]

French syndicalists saw the tactic of sabotage as having primarily three forms: active disablement of machinery or damage of goods, open-mouth—exposure of fraudulent commercial practices—and passive obstructionism.

Passive forms of direct action in the teens typically took the form of the irritation strike also known as "la greve perlee" (pearl strike). The irritation strike was made famous by French railroad workers who changed the routing addresses stuck to the sides of railroad cars for a period of several months. The cars, it was said, were as hard to find as pearls that had dropped off a necklace. Passive resistance could also involve the most minute observation of rules, harassment of functionaries of the employers of labor and complete suspension of initiative and ingenuity. Passive resistance mixed with sabotage, in the lexicon of Wobbly strike culture, was the "folded arms" strike. Trautmann wrote that the earliest example of such a strike was in Cincinnati in 1884. At the Jackson Brewery workers occupied the Schalander, locked the employer out and held off the militia by building barricades out of barrels filled with beer and water to win their strike. The combination of direct action and sabotage (defined as "the withdrawal of efficiency from work") represented the IWW's alternative to the European syndicalists' notion of the general strike as a universal panacea. Eventually this combination developed into the tactic of "striking on the job," foreshadowing the sitdown strikes of the 1930s (a tactic which had in fact already been used by the IWW in a strike against General Electric in 1907).[24]

Walker C. Smith: Smokeless Powder of the Social War

Like many Wobblies active in the pre-World-War-I period, Walker, C. Smith's life history is largely unknown. It is difficult to say precisely when he was exposed to anarchism, or what experiences made him an ardent direct-actionist, In the September 1909 issue of the *Industrial Worker (I.W.)* he is listed as the secretary of IWW mixed local No. 26 in Denver, Colorado, He seems to have used Denver as a home base for several years and in 1911 became involved with anti-militarist agitation against American intervention in the Mexican revolution,[25] Prior to assuming editorship of the *I.W.* in February of 1912, Smith had contributed news articles, essays, and poems to Solidarity and the *I.W.* In January of 1913 Smith initiated a series of thirteen articles on sabotage in the *I.W.* the series with a few revisions was reprinted as a pamphlet in December 1913.

In July 1913 the G.E.B. abruptly fired Smith as editor of the *I.W.* and arbitrarily appointed John F. Leheney, then in Minneapolis, as "acting editor." The factors that led to Smith's dismissal were part of a larger, poorly understood conflict within IWW history between centralizers and decentralizers. The G.E.B.'s actions were bitterly protested by West Coast locals who boycotted the *I.W.* immediately cancelling their bundle orders and refusing to pay debts on bundles already received. Despite efforts by Minneapolis locals, few locals responded to the economic crisis precipitated by the actions of the Western locals and the *I.W.* folded after four issues, resuming publication in April 1916. Following Smith's dismissal, members of the joint local in Spokane, Washington elected him as their secretary and voted to distribute *Social War* and *The Lumberjack* in lieu of the *I.W.* claiming "a triumph for decentralization and an unmuzzled press."[26]

Smith based his sabotage editorials and pamphlet on a translation of Emile Pouget's book *Sabotage*, made available to him by Albin Braida. Making use of Pouget's book, Smith applied the lessons of French syndicalism to American conditions. His pamphlet is replete with examples of how waiters, cooks, farm hands, track gangs, building laborers, factory workers, and others in the U.S. had used the practice to their advantage. Smith did not make apologies for sabotage in any of its forms. He argued that the destruction of property, whether for protection or revenge, showed workers' disregard for the master class's moral code; property, he argued, had no rights that its creators were bound to respect. "The main concern to the revolutionist," Smith argued, "is whether the use of sabotage will destroy the power of the masters in such a way as to give the worker a greater measure of industrial control."

Smith likened sabotage to guerrilla warfare. Whether the secret action of an individual or the mass action of a group, sabotage required courage, initiative, daring, resoluteness, audacity and sacrifice. Those who practiced sabotage were "the sharpshooters of the revolution." In the fight against capitalism, sabotage was like a "smokeless powder. It scores a hit," Smith wrote, "while its source is seldom detected."

Elizabeth Gurley Flynn: Dynamiting the Silk

Elizabeth Gurley Flynn was born in Concord, New Hampshire in 1890, the daughter of immigrant Irish revolutionaries, Thomas and Annie (Gurley) Flynn. Flynn's major radicalizing influences came from her immediate family, from Irish freedom fighters such as James Larkin, Tom Mann and James Connolly who stayed with the Flynns while on their American sojourns, and from her high-school sweetheart Fred Robinson, whose father Dr. William Robinson was a well known anarchist and birth control advocate. She joined IWW mixed Local No. 179 in New York City in 1906, quitting high school a year later to devote herself full time to IWW activities. At age seventeen she was elected a delegate to the IWW's third convention in 1907 and made her first speaking tour for the IWW on her way back from Chicago.[27]

Flynn was a key organizer in the IWW's free-speech fights in Missoula, Montana and Spokane, Washington between 1908 and 1910, the Lawrence textile strike of 1912, the Paterson silk strike in 1913, the Mesabi range strike of 1916, and the Passaic textile strike of 1926. Of Flynn's skill as an orator, her longtime friend Mary Heaton Vorse, feminist and pioneer labor journalist, wrote:

> When Elizabeth Gurley Flynn spoke, the excitement of the crowd became a visible thing. She stood there, young, with her Irish blue eyes, her face magnolia white and her cloud of black hair, the picture of a youthful revolutionary girl leader. She stirred them, lifted them up in her appeal for solidarity. Then at the end of the meeting they sang. It was as though a spurt of flame had gone through the audience, something stirring and powerful, a feeling which had made the liberation of the people possible, something beautiful and strong had swept through the people and welded them together, singing.[28]

Flynn's skill as an orator is especially seen in *Sabotage: The Conscious Withdrawal of the Workers' Industrial Efficiency*, a speech she made during the 1913 Paterson silk strike. Her speech was printed as a pamphlet in 1915, by the IWW's Cleveland Publishing Bureau, supposedly without the G.E.B.'s permission. Following the Cleveland chapter's dissolution in 1916, the pamphlet was temporarily withdrawn from circulation by the G.E.B., but was reprinted in 1917—this time over Flynn's objections.

Her speech focused on methods of striking popularized by French and British syndicalists—the "old-fashioned working class practices from time immemorial," and gave examples of their creative application in the U.S. She discussed the use of sabotage by employer to increase profits, the hypocrisy of the legal system and consequences for consumers. She exposed the deceitful practice of "dynamiting" silk, a method in which manufacturers added metals such as zinc, tin and lead and salt to increase the weight of silk. Through this method the manufacturer used one pound of pure silk in order to net from three to fifteen pounds. This affected the durability of fabrics made of silk, causing them to crack or fall apart. "Non-adulteration," Flynn said in her speech, "is the highest form of sabotage in an establishment like the dye house of Paterson, bakeries, confectioners, meat packing houses, restaurants, etc."

Flynn had originally made this speech to lend support to New York socialist and IWNC member Frederick Sumner Boyd. Boyd was arrested and later convicted of "advising destruction of property" in a speech made to Paterson silk workers. He advised workers who found their coworkers replaced by scabs to add chemicals to the dyeing process which would "render the silk unweavable and to use vinegar on the reed of the loom to prevent its operation." When Boyd's appeal failed he was sent to the state prison at Trenton to serve a two to seven years sentence. As Flynn's pamphlet was about to go to press, Boyd signed a petition for pardon in which he renounced the advocacy of sabotage and all "other subversive ideas." Since it was too late to change the many references to Boyd in the pamphlet, an explanation appears on the final page noting Boyd's "cowardice." In her autobiography Flynn went further suggesting that Boyd may have been a provocateur. Flynn, however, was also to renounce her earlier enthusiasm for sabotage. Indicted under the Espionage Act in 1917, she wrote an appeal to President Wilson asking him to intervene and clear her of the unjust charges:

> The only conceivable basis for my indictment is a pamphlet on "sabotage" written four years ago in defense of men arrested during the Paterson strike. I had no intention that it should apply to any other time or conditions than those of which I wrote, and long before my arrest had requested that the IWW not publish it further until I could rewrite it.[29]

The letter, which was part of her successful strategy to separate her case from other Wobblies indicted under the Espionage Act, deepened an already existing rift with Secretary-Treasurer Bill Haywood, and foreshadowed her departure from the IWW. Following a long illness, Flynn later renewed her activism, becoming a major figure in labor defense work and helping to shape and direct the strategies in many major battles over workers' political rights during the first third of the twentieth century. Flynn was a co-founder of the American Civil Liberties Union in 1920, was active with the Workers Defense League (1918–1924), International Labor Defense (1918–1926) and the Garland Fund (1925–1926). Through her work with the Workers Defense League she helped defend the rights of victims of the Palmer Raids and to organize protests against the Ku Klux Klan. In later years she was primarily active in the Communist Party.[30]

Conclusion

The resurgence of direct action and sabotage in the early 1910s opposed the new industrial efficiency ("scientific management") and the repressive tactics used by the state and big business to defeat labor strikes. The tactics of direct action and sabotage re-emerged within a movement culture that sought to regain control over the labor process. Workers used these tactics to organize across workplace boundaries, to create forms of self-organization that were empowering, and to build community. The movement affirmed a new identity and purpose for marginalized and disfranchised workers living at the edges of survival, and initiated new alliances.

The legacy of the revolutionary industrial union movement, and of the tactics that were part of its strike culture, is complex. Part of this legacy is the repression directed against its strike culture. This repression not only continues to be employed against labor, but has grown in scope and brutality. The wave of repression that began during World War I was directed against the IWWs anti-war activities, and associated the tactic of direct action with domestic violence and plots to sabotage the "war effort." These charges, however, were never substantiated, in spite of lengthy trials that followed mass arrests. After extensive research, a scholar observed in 1939:

> Although there are contradictory opinions as to whether the IWW practices sabotage or not, it is interesting to note that no case of an IWW saboteur caught practicing sabotage or convicted of its practice is available.[31]

The more salient part of the legacy is the form of solidarity created by workers acting on their own initiative against social injustice. This solidarity and the culture it created emerged at a critical moment in the history of the labor movement. These tactics emerged at a time when the "official" organized labor movement was spiritually and politically bankrupt, and when corporate power again threatened the survival of millions of workers.

Not the least significant part of this Wobbly strike culture's legacy lies in its appealing lyrics and visual imagery. Numerous indeed are the songs, cartoons, and "silent agitator" stickers inspired by direct action and sabotage—the "sab-o-tabby kitten," the black cat and "the good old wooden shoe." Much of the best work of Joe Hill/Ralph Chaplin, Ernest Riebe, Covington Hall, T-Bone Slim and other IWW songsters and cartoonists is devoted to these themes.

Following the waves of repression directed at the IWW in the late 1910s and '20s, the struggle for industrial unionism and the tactic of direct action re-emerged in the 1930s. The IWW was a very small union in those years, but its influence persisted. Here and there—along the Gulf Coast, for example, as well as in Yakima, Detroit, and Cleveland—the IWW enjoyed brief moments of resurgence. More durably, Individual Wobblies and ex-Wobs played important roles in the rise of the Congress of Industrial Organizations (CIO), especially in the United Auto Workers, but also in mining and maritime.

In several independent unions, the IWW's impact was much greater. The activities of Frank Ellis in building the Independent Union of All Workers (IUAW) provides an interesting example of the endurance of the spirit and tactics of Wobbly strike culture, as well as an approach that has great relevance today. Ellis had served on the IWW's General Executive Board in the early 1920s, and was later indicted for "criminal syndicalism" in Omaha. A skilled "boomer" butcher, he worked in meatpacking plants throughout the Midwest. In the early 1930s he began organizing in the Hormel plant in Austin, Minnesota, along with a handful of other labor activists, including Minneapolis Trotskyists Carl Skoglund and Ray Dunne. As labor historian Peter Rachleff noted in his work on the union,

> the IUAW relied on visible workplace confrontations to build the union. . . . They not only demonstrated their strength to the company but also demonstrated the workers' own strength to themselves. Direct Action remained the preeminent tactic.

The IUAW is credited with the first sitdown strike of the 1930s. From its base in the Austin Hormel plant, the IUAW organized locals all over Minnesota and Iowa as well as in North and South Dakota and Wisconsin. In many places, the IUAW not only spread industrial unionism among packing house workers, but also the strategy of organizing "wall to wall"—that is, setting a goal of 100% unionization in those communities. In Austin the IUAW local ranged from units of truckers and warehouse workers to beauty shops of three employees to Montgomery Ward's.[32]

Another Wobbly-influenced independent union that started in the 1930s, and whose experience is still relevant today, is the multiracial Southern Tenant Farmers' Union (STFU), the first fully integrated union in the modern South. Organized by eighteen black and white sharecroppers in Tyronza, Arkansas in 1934, within five years the STFU was organizing all through the South and its membership numbered in the tens of thousands. In his 1987 pictorial history of the union, *Roll the Union On*, STFU co-founder H.L. Mitchell emphasized its direct-action orientation.

In an interview with Franklin Rosemont the following year, Mitchell specified the STFU's affinities with the IWW:

> First, it was our purpose to help workers organize themselves, rather than for us to organize them. In the STFU we never told anyone what to do. At our meetings . . . everyone who wanted to would state his or her views, there'd be a discussion and then the workers would do what they wanted. This kind of real union democracy . . . was something vital that we shared with the IWW.
>
> Direct action was another thing we and the Wobblies had in common. . . . Ninety-nine percent of our members couldn't vote anyway, because of the poll tax, so we had to figure out our own ways of doing things. All the great things done by the STFU were started by the workers in the ranks . . . In 1936, twenty years before Eisenhower sent U.S. troops to desegregate Little Rock, Arkansas, we desegregated the hotels and

restaurants there during our Convention. We didn't ask anybody's permission. We just went ahead and did it.

The STFU shared the IWW's notion that a union's strength rests in its membership, not in its treasury. We never had any money, but we did great things anyway. . . . Enthusiasm is what counts.[33]

These IWW pamphlets from the 1910s are reprinted here to reaffirm this spirit of rank-and-file initiative and solidarity at a time when direct-action tactics are again stimulating debate. Action on the part of indigenous peoples throughout the world, anti-racists, environmental groups such as Earth First!, animal rights activists, the homeless, computer hackers, pirate radio broadcasters, as well as self-organization by rank-and-file workers and community struggles for self-determination are again challenging us to rethink these tactics. In recent years we have seen direct action at work in the coal pits of Pittston, in the redwood forests on the Pacific coast, in the refusal of dockworkers to unload boats with goods from apartheid South Africa, in the new wave of French sit-down strikes, in the massive general strike in Korea, and in the global resistance of indigenous peoples against the destruction of the Earth's resources.

Direct action is recognized as a valuable and effective tactic by many movements, and remains a cutting edge tool for social change. Whenever communities in struggle find more conventional methods of resistance closed to them, direct action and sabotage will be employed.

Salvatore Salerno

NOTES

1. Staughton Lynd, ed. *Nonviolence in America: A Documentary History* (Indianapolis: Bobbs-Merrill, 1966), 217–241.
2. K.G.J.C. Knowles. *Strikes: A Study in Industrial Conflict* (N.Y.: Philosophical Library, 1952), 1–2.
3. C.L.R. James, "The Atlantic Slave Trade and Slavery: Some Interpretations of Their Significance in the Development of the U.S. and the Western World," in *Amistad I: Writings on Black History and Culture*, edited by John A. Williams and Charles F. Harris (N.Y.: Vintage Books, 1970), 126–129, 135. Robin D.G. Kelley, *Race Rebels: Culture, Politics and the Black Working Class* (N.Y.: Free Press, 1994), 20–21.
4. James Joll, *The Anarchists* (Cambridge, Mass.: Harvard University Press, 1979), 104.
5. E.P. Thompson, *The Making of the English Working Class* (N.Y.: Vintage Books, 1966), 62–63. See also Kelley, *Race Rebels*, Chapter 1.
6. Pierre Dubois, *Sabotage in Industry* (N.Y.: Penguin Books, 1979), 98–99.
7. Christian Cornelissen, "Uber den Internationalen Syndikalismus," *Archiv fur Sozialwissenshaft*, XXX (Jan. 1910), translated in *Industrial Worker*, 18 June 1910, 2, as "Origins of Syndicalism." See also Rudolf Rocker, *Anarcho-Syndicalism* (London: Secker and Warburg, 1938), 56–81, and Robert Hunter, *Violence and the Labor Movement* (N.Y.: Macmillan, 1914), 154–193.
8. Paul Avrich, "Bakunin and the United States," *International Review of Social History*, 24 (1979), 333; Donald D. Egbert and Stow Parsons, eds., *Socialism and American Life* (Princeton, N.J.: Princeton University Press, 1952), 234–235.
9. G. M. Stekloff, *History of the First International* (London: Martin Lawrence, 1928), 258.
10. Cornelissen, "Origins of Syndicalism"; Salvatore Salerno, *Red November, Black November: Culture and Community in the IWW* (N.Y.: State University of New York Press, 1989), 51–53.
11. Ibid.

12. Emile Pouget, *Sabotage*, translated from the French and introduced by Arturo Giovannitti (Chicago: Charles H. Kerr, 1913), 41–42; Andre Tridon, *The New Unionism* (N.Y.: B.W. Huebsch, 1917), 37–38.

13. Franklin Rosemont, "Introduction" to Ernest Riebe, *Mr. Block: Twenty-Four IWW Cartoons* (Chicago: Charles H. Kerr, 1984; a reprint of an IWW comic book first published in 1913), 6.

14. Pouget, *Sabotage*, 41–42.

15. Rudolf Rocker, *Johann Most: Das Leben eines Rebellen* (Germany: Verlag Detlev Auvermann, 1973), 394.

16. For an insightful discussion of the "short shovels" story see Archie Green, *Wobblies, Pile Butts, and Other Heroes: Laborlore Explorations* (Chicago: University of Illinois Press, 1993). 327–341. On the Paterson anarchists, see George W. Carey. "The Vessel, The Deed and The Idea: The Paterson Anarchists, 1895–1908," unpublished manuscript, 248–286.

17. Sally M. Miller, *The Radical Immigrant* (N.Y.: Twayne, 1974), 108; Gary M. Fink et al., *Biographical Dictionary of American Labor Leaders* (Westport, Conn.: Greenwood, 1974), 358–359; Salerno, *Red November, Black November*, 59–60.

18. Don K. McKee, "The Influences of Syndicalism Upon DeLeon," *The Historian* 20 (May 1958), 284. See also Salvatore Salerno, "The Impact of Haymarket on the Founding of the NMI," in Dave Roediger and Franklin Rosemont, eds., *Haymarket Scrapbook* (Chicago: Charles H. Kerr, 1986), 190–191.

19. Ira Kipnis, *The American Socialist Movement, 1897–1912* (N.Y.: Columbia University Press, 1952), 195.

20. "Two Views of Sabotage," *Solidarity*, 25 February 1912, 4.

21. Fred W. Thompson, *The IWW: Its First Fifty Years* (Chicago: IWW, 1955), 87.

22. Kipnis, *The American Socialist Movement*, 415–417.

23. William E. Trautmann, *Direct Action and Sabotage* (Pittsburgh: Socialist News Co., 1912), 21–22. Trautmann's other pamphlets include *Industrial Unionism: New Methods and New Forms* (Chicago: Charles H. Kerr, 1909), and *Why Strikes*

Are Lost (Chicago: IWW, c. 1911); the latter is reprinted in
Joyce L. Kornbluh, ed., *Rebel Voices: An IWW Anthology*
(Chicago: Charles H. Kerr, 1988). See also David Roediger's
important analysis of sabotage in the Brotherhood of
Timber Workers, "Gaining a Hearing for Black-White Unity:
Covington Hall and the Complexities of Race, Gender and
Class," in his *Towards the Abolition of Whiteness* (N.Y.: Verso,
1994).

24. William E. Trautmann, "Power of Folded Arms and Thinking
Bayonets." Typescript, IWW Collection, Box 146, Folder 17,
Labor History Archive, Wayne State University, 5–7.

25. *Industrial Worker*, 23 September 1909, 4; "Anti-Military Stickers,"
I.W., 11 May 1911, 4. See also Box-Car Bertha, *Sister of the
Road: The Autobiography of Box-Car Bertha as Told to Dr. Ben
Reitman* (N.Y.: Harper & Row, 1975), 11–12 and 124–131.

26. Thomas McEnroe, "IWW Theories, Organizational Problems
and Appeals as Revealed in the *Industrial Worker*." Ph.D.
dissertation, University of Minnesota, 1960, 36–44; "Triumph
for Decentralization," *I.W.*, 14 August 1913, 2.

27. Rosalyn Fraad Baxandall, *Words on Fire: The Life and Writings
of Elizabeth Gurley Flynn* (New Brunswick: N.J.: Rutgers
University Press, 1989), 2–8.

28. Ibid., 17.

29. Ibid.

30. Ibid., 23–27.

31. Eldridge Foster Dowell, *History of Criminal Syndicalism
Legislation in the United States* (Baltimore: Johns Hopkins
University Studies in Historical and Political Science, Series
LVI, No. 1, 1939), 36.

32. Peter Rachleff, "Organizing 'Wall to Wall': The Independent
Union of All Workers, 1933–37," in Staughton Lynd, ed., *"We
Are All Leaders": The Alternative Unionism of the Early 1930s*
(Chicago: University of Illinois Press, 1996), 51–71. See also
Rachleff's *Hard Pressed in the Heartland: The Hormel Strike
and the Future of the Labor Movement* (Boston: South End

Press, 1993).

33.   H.L. Mitchell, *Roll the Union On: A Pictorial History of the Southern Tenant Farmers' Union* (Chicago: Charles H. Kerr, 1987); Franklin Rosemont, "The IWW and the STFU: An Interview with H.L. Mitchell," in the *Industrial Worker* (Chicago, April 1988), 7.

DIRECT ACTION AND SABOTAGE

By WM. E. TRAUTMAN   PRICE 10 CENTS

Socialist News Co.
342 Third Avenue   Pittsburgh, Pa.

Cartoon by Ern Hanson

Silent Agitator Sticker
by Ralph Chaplin (circa 1916)

Direct Action and Sabotage
William E. Trautmann

AWFUL! AN AWFUL THING!

A STREET SPEAKER, ONCE BEING ASKED BY A BYSTANDER, was pressed to answer whether the socialists approved of direct action and sabotage. "Oh no, no, they are opposed to it, they are denouncing it, it is an anarchist doctrine." Again the persistent bystander put the question. "What then is direct action, what is sabotage? It should be explained if so repulsive as a weapon of the workers in the warfare against the capitalist class."—"Destruction of human life by dynamite, of property with powder and other explosives, repetitions of McNamara outrages," was the cocksure reply. The crowd yelled approval, the craft unionists in that crowd nodded their heads as an impressive demonstration that the trades union principals were not to be held responsible for the McNamaras. A labor fakir or two yelled themselves hoarse exclaiming: "Gompers and the American Federation of Labor disapprove such methods as direct action and sabotage, it's the illegitimate organization, the Industrial Workers of the World, that preaches the use of direct action and sabotage, they ought to be outlawed." And a lonely member of the Socialist Labor Party added to it: "It's Haywood and his gang of anarchists who advocate

'Direct Action,' and other uncivilized methods, and therefore we of the Detroit Socialist Labor Party have repudiated them."

And these assurances by the "intellectual" fountain heads of the labor movement are passed unchallenged, and travel all over the country as indisputable facts. They form the basis for discussions and resolutions, and in the official records of many a body of workers these terms of "direct action" and "sabotage" are inscribed as meaning something that must be tabooed.

The matter is thus settled, until papers occasionally bring it to the notice of millions, for instance, that striking mine workers, in that or the other district, got the mine engineers and pumpmen to strike with them, and that as a result mines were flooded and could not be operated for weeks.

"Oh, that's right," says the street shouter this time; "all workers must quit together, and when Mr. Capitalist sees that there are no workers to protect property against deterioration by other than human efforts then he will soon squeal and give in." And in this apparent contradiction lies the admission that few only understand what "direct action" and "sabotage" really mean, what they imply, what forces are needed for their operation, what results are expected to be attained by the use of these methods, and it is only hoped that this treatise of the subject will be enlarged by others who are as staunch advocates of these methods as the author of this pamphlet is.

INDIRECT AND DIRECT ACTION.

"The economic power of the capitalist class, used by that class for the oppression of labor . . . in the nature of things can not be radically changed, or even slightly amended for the benefit of the working people, except through the direct action of the working people themselves, economically and politically united as a class."

—From the Preamble of the S.T. and L.A.

In this true statement of objects, the S.T. and L.A. proclaimed itself as the first labor organization which advocated direct action as the principal, as the only, method by which the economic power of the capitalist class could be radically changed or even slightly amended by the workers organized as a class.

But if the workers are supposed to organize as a class it presupposes that there must be another class. The latter, by the very nature of things, seeks to prevent this radical change or slight amelioration of conditions based on their economic power. This class, the capitalists, are secured in their economic power by the ownership of land, mines, factories and transportation utilities. These possessions, though, have no value in themselves. Human labor power must be applied to these economic resources before they yield value, and thereby also assure power to one class to determine the relationship of the other class who invest their labor power in these industrial possessions. This human labor power is obtained from the millions of toilers, for wages. Wages, though, only represent a small proportion of the value of a product created by the application of human efforts. The job of the workers in these economic possessions is the privilege to work for wages, and the job itself is an inseparable and indispensable part of the economic possessions of the employing class, and consequently also of their economic power.

This direct ownership of economic resources and control of economic power would oft be open to dispute. Therefore, infringements upon that domain of power must be prevented at all hazards. For this object political institutions are maintained and used to protect this industrial power of the capitalist class, with the aid of courts, police, militia, jails and legislative institutions.

The applied labor power of the working class is the most indispensable part of that economic power wielded by the employing class. Without that there would be no production, and without production there would be no economic power at all.

The workers instinctively, and millions now consciously, feel that they alone contribute to the making of this economic power for the class of non-producers. And they, consequently, strive to wrest that economic power away from the employing class, with means and methods that are either direct or indirect.

In these endeavors the workers meet, as a matter of course, the fierce opposition of the owners of economic resources and the wielders of economic power. And as the political institutions are operated to protect the latter in their power they use them to subdue any attempt to question, or efforts to infringe upon their domain of possessions and economic supremacy. They use the indirect methods of the agencies of legislation and institutions for the execution of their mandates and laws. Parliaments, courts, militia, police are used to prevent successful withdrawal, if possible, of the human laboring forces, which form the most indispensable part of their economic power, from the operation of the mechanical or other devices. Or they use them in the maintenance of their economic possessions to offer jobs to those who would not infringe upon their absolute domain, and who patiently acknowledge the employer's sovereignty over the life conditions of the millions who must have a job to live, the job, which though, forms the basic source of economic power for the oppression of the many, by the few.

The capitalist class uses the "indirect" method of political repression to check, if possible, direct actions on the part of the workers, that is, the withdrawal of their labor power and also their efficiency, from the workshops, the mines, land, etc. Only when he is assured of the use of that political agency in his behalf will he resort also to the direct action method, to wit: Throw the disgruntled workers out by a lockout.

Concluding from these observances that these political institutions and their consistent use for the purpose for which they were created, are the sole causes for the abuses and wrongs the workers suffer in the places of production, political reformers would advocate the capture of the political institutions. It is the easiest way of resisting the cruel abuse of political power. The workers, in large numbers, are told to base their hope in the change of the economic conditions on the application of indirect means, so to reach thereby, so they are told, the foundation of the economic power of the employing class. Political institutions in the control of the working class, and used for their own purposes, are hailed as the instruments by which the economic possession and industrial power of the capitalist class can be infringed upon and finally be overthrown. The conquest of political power is therefore, according to these statesmen, a prerequisite for effectually contesting the domain of economic power of the employers of labor, the job-owning class.

But political institutions are dependencies of economic possessions, and the political actions and the struggle for political positions for avowed purposes are therefore "indirect actions." For the materialization of such "indirect actions" organized efforts are necessary, and these organized efforts find their expression and combined strength in political organizations. The political organization of the working class, for instance, if it is to be a class organization, would therefore be a reflex only of the desire to gain control of the political institutions, the object being to wield them for purposes diametrically opposed to the economic interests of those holding the economic power by their possession of the means of production, exchange and the means of employment of wage labor, which, as shown before, constitutes the most indispensable part of the economic possessions of the capitalist class.

But in observing actual conditions and occurrences the workers perceive how the capitalists shut down plants, either by lockouts and or by compulsory suspensions as consequences of industrial panics, or as the result of the concentration process in industries and their management. In these cases the economic possessions deteriorate in value, even are void of any market value, as long as factories are not kept running and machines and other devices are not longer operated by human hands and supervised by human ingenuity.

Is it any wonder, therefore, that from the days that production by collective combination began, the workers became conscious of the important part they formed in the process of production? The job in the workshops, mines, farms and transportation instruments was the indispensable factor in the economic power of the capitalist class. The withdrawal from the job, the suspension of operation, the withdrawal of efficiency from that position of employment were therefore methods that suggested themselves as more direct, as aiming straight to the point and curtailing the economic power of the capitalist class, and thereby also reducing the efficiency of the political institutions wielded by them for the protection of their interests.

Those direct action methods are grouped and determined in their application according to the conditions in the various industries and industrial combinations. But not always are "direct actions" inaugurated for the social protection and advancement of the working class. The capitalists, quite often, knowing the immense power that the wage workers place in their own hands for the oppression of the working class, engage the direct actions of workers for the furthering of their own plans. Only when "direct actions" are applied in efforts to undermine the economic power of the employing class, are they essentially and socially useful and beneficial, no matter whether they are "direct actions" of individuals, or of combinations of workers.

SOCIAL AND ANTI-SOCIAL DIRECT ACTION.

The suppression of the rights of free speech, free assemblage and combination breeds the determination to apply direct action methods in their most violent forms. And their application is justified by such conditions, inevitably. The Russian individualist who uses explosives, responsible only to himself as an individual, may be abhorred by many, but still his action must be judged by the results he aims to achieve. If ultimately, after a long series of such violent and destructive direct actions they result in the removal of agencies of suppression and oppression his direct action is socially useful.

But when the Russian autocracy uses agents and hirelings to impose on these individuals responsible to themselves only, and exploits them, unconsciously to themselves, for the furtherance of their own obscure and criminal designs, then the results, stamp such acts as anti-social direct actions.

In the possessions of the United States Steel Corporation, Jones and Laughlin, and others, the workers are denied, absolutely, the right to seek redress against appalling wrongs by organized efforts. The methods of repression are worse than those applied in most backward countries. Individual self-help is therefore an inevitable method to look for redress and the righting of wrongs.

One actual occurrence, out of hundreds that occur every year in the possessions of these corporations, will illustrate the point quite clearly. A former graduate of the Moscow university was compelled to escape the fangs of the Bloody Czar. Shortly after landing in America, he found employment in the Pressed Steel Car Company plant at McKees Rocks. The second strike in 1910 forced him out of employment. R...... went to Chicago and got a job in the Rolling mill of the United States Steel Corporation in Gary, Ind. There, as a common laborer, despite a university education, working twelve hours a day, he encountered the ill-will of an ignorant straw boss. The ignorant brutes employed by the corporations as overseers and bosses cannot bear to see an intelligent-looking face among the hordes of humanity who patiently and meekly bow to their tyrannic, overbearing commands and appalling impositions. The boss would make it hard for this worker, sneer at him, call him epithets to which the steel workers are getting well-nigh accustomed (they don't mind them any more). But this boss being treated by R...... with silent contempt, threw one day, by sheer accident, a heavy hammer on R......'s feet. Laid up in Gary's Corporation hospital for weeks, and lucky to get out alive from that slaughter house, he went back to work and was, without protest on his part, assigned to the same job he occupied before, and under the same foreman. The latter would continue his abuses, until one day the foreman stood again in the gangway on which the workers drive on cranes the white heated ingots into the roll. He was purposely obstructing the road to force R...... who was due with his steel block, to switch aside when passing him. But the latter, purposely not noticing the boss drove the heavy ingot against the brute, and accidently the ingot fell upon the foreman, as accidently as he threw the hammer on the victim's feet, only that the last mentioned accident cost the foreman's life. Was this an act socially justifiable or not?

Let it be considered, according to best information and close personal observation, that half of these fatal accidents in the mills, in which human rights are completely ignored and suppressed, are the result of "individual direct actions." But it is certain also, that these actions suggest to thousands the application of more effective combined protest and resistance. And as the organized revolt is only the result of the series of individual direct actions, the latter under such conditions and in similar cases must be classified as socially beneficent and are therefore "social direct actions."

But, conversely, when human lives are sacrificed as a result of a combination of interests who further plans which, in the long run, are detrimental to the working class as a whole, though groups of them may derive immediate benefits, then the conclusion is different. When the Fuller Construction Company, backed by the Steel Trust, squeezed its competitors to the wall by using the Craft Unions of their employees, and their officials, to apply occasionally the most "explosive and violent direct action methods" it was, from the viewpoint of class-conscious workers, anti-social direct action. And when after this task had been accomplished, the Steel Trust set out to annihilate that same union that had been once so useful to them, and when the latter combined with other groups of manufacturers to stem the wave of destruction, and when, as a result thereof, the dynamite explosions blew out the life of workers who were not parties to these contests between former allies and later rivals, then this result must be judged from the effects it created on the entire working-class struggle to obtain possession and control of the job. The means, the end were detrimental, anti-social, criminal, and must therefore be classified under anti-social "direct actions."

In all these cases, however, we see "direct action," be it social or anti-social in character, applied by individuals. The destructive violent tendencies they often develop, are the results and the revolt against anti-social conditions. Whenever and wherever the industrial situation necessitates the amassing of large bodies of workers in given places, the individual is soon submerged in that great mass. But this mass would remain stagnant, stoic, were it not for the "actions" of individuals in a series of attacks against unbearable conditions. They are the yeast in the leaven preparing the cells for an amalgamation into compact material. In the long run these "individual direct actions" shatter the stability of capitalist absolute control of the job, the source of their economic power. Conversely, the self-assertions of individuals comes to an end when the masses begin to move. The masses in their claims and struggles against wrongs and repressions beget the mass efforts and mass organizations.

But the existence of mass organizations and mass efforts does not necessarily imply that they are to be used as levers for the attainment of things socially good for the working class in its entirety. Mass organizations, in the application of "direct actions" can not always, by the nature of their objects, refrain from the use of violent and destructive methods. As long as the mass is not imbued with that spirit which is generated by the recognition of a fierce class struggle in the social system for the control of the jobs, they may be goaded on to perpetrate acts which, in their relation to the working class and working-class movement in general determines the character.

Ignorance of the real cause of their lack of economic power, and the source of power of the employing class, is mostly the reason why mass organizations of workers are using direct action methods for anti-social purposes.

Reprehensive operation of mass efforts by designing agents of capitalist interests, to further the ends of the latter in solidifying and strengthening their own economic power, furnishes another reason why in final results such use of direct and also indirect action methods must be classified as anti-social in character, and therefore, by the very nature of things, detrimental to working-class interests.

RESULTS ALONE DETERMINE CHARACTER OF MASS ACTIONS.

It matters not whether these mass organizations call themselves Mechanics' Unions, or Knights of Labor, American Labor Union, Molly Maguires, Trades Unions, Industrial Unions, Syndicalist organizations or what else, they all have been formed for the use of "direct actions" and only accidently have been used for purely political indirect actions, much to their own undoing and disintegration.

But whether these mass movements, resulting in mass actions on direct lines, have been guided by a desire to radically change or slightly amend the conditions making for the oppression of labor, must be judged by the intelligent application of the methods at their disposal, and what the results were which they sought to obtain, or attained.

The Molly Maguires, in their resistance against aggression, thought that they had an exclusive right to the jobs in the mines, with the exclusion of all other nationalities. Stubborn as was their fight, ending only with the judicial assassination of innocent workers, yet they were used, because of this narrowness, by the capitalists and their henchmen, to wage war on another portion of wage workers, and therefore, their "direct action" methods were anti-social. The Knights of Labor, and the Railroad Workers organized with them, then had many hard skirmishes with the capitalists who consciously knew that the workers were aiming at a larger control of their job conditions; indirectly, therefore, at the curtailment of economic power of the master class. Methods were used, quite often, which resulted in destruction and devastation. But as long as they directed their direct action methods against the capitalists, the world of workers did not object, even encouraged them. The final results, as long as this policy of attacking the capitalist class alone was pursued, were socially good for the entire working class. When later the economic strength of these workers was used for the support and enlargement of political powers of the capitalists, the economic basis of the organizations gave way, and in the final end their actions became decidedly anti-social. Another mass organization noteworthy in this connection is the American Railway Union. Direct actions marked the career of the organization in its advent to economic power. Even when, after the Pullman strike, it appeared that it had failed in all its objects, it was never denied that by its use of the direct action road it had acquired great social good for hundred thousands of workers. It failed when it left its economic foundation and switched from the clear path into a political party camp. Anti-social were the final effects of both the gigantic struggles of the Knights of Labor and the American Railway Union, when the capitalists, seeing how the basis of their own economic power had been successfully threatened, again safeguarded themselves against repetitions by their open support of the craft union movement, and the misdirection of the actions of the workers for purposes that were in no way dangerous to the interests of the capitalists, even protective in the perpetuation of the foundation for their economic possessions and power.

But the craft unions also use methods which can be classified as "direct actions." They apparently are also formed out of the mass for mass actions and efforts. This we will later investigate. First we must find what are the methods of "direct action," what of "indirect action."

DIRECT ACTION INSTRUMENTS.

The strike is undoubtedly the best instrument of direct action. By it the workers withdraw, in smaller or larger masses, their producing power from the job, the basis of the economic power of the employing class. The strike may be confined to a shop, or separate industries, but when it involves an industry, (no matter in what locality situated), of all workers, it then becomes a mass strike. When the workers in all or most of the industries in a given district or locality are involved then it is a "general strike." And if it appears that the solidarity of labor commands them to withdraw their labor power from all the instruments of production in a given country then it is a "Universal Strike."

Irritation strikes are sporadic strikes, during which the workers quit for a while their jobs, return to work for a given period until the industry or plant is in normal working order, then withdraw again spontaneously and without notice, in constant repetition until their objects are obtained.

Destructive Strikes, in the beginning of which machinery is destroyed and the operation system is so demoralized that a resumption of work is only possible after the damaged tools are repaired or replaced and the operating machinery put in order again, are usually noted by the absence of any organization.

INDIRECT ACTIONS.

Political action is indirect, most of the time. The object is to secure control of political agencies, the reflex of economic power, and wield them to prevent the agencies of capitalist production from abusing their privileges, to the detriment of those who are striving with all means at their command to establish their partial, and ultimately complete control and possession of the job, the basis of all economic and political power. This is the most that even ardent advocates of political action can expect to obtain. When, for the maintenance or contest for political rights direct actions are invoked, as for instance in general strikes for the equal suffrage, it only proves that these indirect actions are void of any results if the economic power of the producers is not organized and wielded to make these slight ameliorations obtained by political, indirect action, permanent in the struggle for the possession of the job.

The boycott is essentially an instrument of "indirect action." By the application of the principle that the purchasers have a right to withdraw the patronage of goods manufactured by certain objectionable manufacturers or distributors, they thereby wish to bring pressure to bear that the workers involved should gain certain conditions in the place of employment, at the job.

Like in the application of indirect political action others than wage workers are expected to contribute to the attainments of certain ends outlined, so is also the boycott one of the means by which with the aid and co-operation of non-workers who are appealed to also, the desired results are to be achieved.

By the passive resistance strike, another means of "indirect action," the workers seek to make the job unprofitable for the master without ever leaving their places of employment. By the most minute observance of rules, and the harassing of the immediate functionaries of the employers of labor, by carrying out the orders with a complete suspension of their own initiative and ingenuity, the workers seek to obtain the same results, the curtailment of the economic power of the employing class in their absolute control of the conditions of employment, and for the establishment of more rights in dictating the terms of sale of their producing power.

The next akin to the passive resistance strike, many times even inoperative without the latter, is the instrument of "sabotage," the most abused and misunderstood term used in the vocabulary of "actions." So much space has been devoted to a discussion and dissection of this subject that a full explanation is not out of place in this presentation of facts and arguments.

CAPITALIST SABOTAGE AND WORKERS' SABOTAGE.

It should be superfluous to tell the workers who read this booklet much about the application of "direct" and "indirect" actions by the capitalists to establish and maintain their sovereignty over the basis of their economic power, the job of the producer, of the workers. The strike, local, general or universal, is answered with the lockout, locally, in industries, universally, if need be, and when they are prepared for it. Irritation strikes they meet with the closing down of their factories or mines in one district and overtaxed operation of their factories and workshops in other districts. Political action by the workers they answer with the withdrawal of the rights of free speech, free assemblage and coalition, and by the use of their servile tools, and the mass they purposely keep in ignorance, for the ratification of their abridgement of political guarantees. They counteract the boycott with their blacklist. The passive resistance for their own purposes is seen from the utter contempt of capitalists for any provisions by which life and limb of the toilers is supposed to be protected. This enforced indifference and silent acquiescence in the mandates of the employers to disregard these provisions has been and is being paid every day by thousands of workers with their life and health and limbs. The criminal passive resistance for capitalist purposes is responsible for such awful disasters as the murder of hundreds in the Cherry mines of Illinois, the Triangle factory slaughter of men, women and innocents. Is it necessary to enumerate all the crimes perpetrated every day, as a result of the passive resistance of the capitalist class against measures that would guarantee security to the human attachment of the job, the toiler?

And as all these "actions" have been the result of observations of the manner in which the employing class uses its economic power, politically and economically organized as a class, to prevent even slight ameliorations, so is the old instrument of indirect action, now termed "sabotage" taken out of the arsenal of the oppressors of labor. In a few illustrations it can be shown how sabotage is in daily use for the enlargement of capitalist profit-interests, and how it, when applied in the opposite direction, turns this instrument of capitalism into a means whereby the workers may effectually gain possession of more economic rights.

A glance over the yearly reports of health and poor food commissions and government inspectors will reveal a few facts to the point. Here we see that millions of eggs are condemned in the store houses. The food commissioners discover that there are "spots" No. 1 and spots No. 2 and "Roses" in the market. These spots and roses, sorted according to the degree that the rosening or rottening process has reached, are used mostly in bakeries for pies and cakes, and bread. The bakery worker knows it, is aware of it since ever bakeshop slaves had to work in dirty, filthy, vermin-infested workshops. His job is supposed to make him immune against the effects of perfumes and deteriorated flour. He has to mix it in so that everybody will believe and think that the bakeshops, small and large, are operated under the most sanitary conditions. So these millions of "spots" are backed in and nicely mixed by the worker in the bakeshop. These cakes and pies are mostly sold to the poorer people, their stomach is hardened anyway by the adulterated stuff they consume every day without knowing it. The effect of this slow poisoning process are scarcely noticed.

But what a howl would go up—in fact, we heard quite often the furor that these statements of plain facts have created—if the bakery workers on a nice day, all together, would announce that the "spots" and "roses" are all in abundant quantity baked into a certain assortment of baked wares. The consumer is warned of the possibilities—who ever gets one of these "rose embalmed" pies is himself only to blame if his stomach gets out of commission. Sabotage applied in the interest of capitalist profit returns is suddenly applied to curtail the returns. It has been done, quite often, and no resolution of protest will stop it either, whenever the workers in the bakeshops are determined to use this "indirect action" instrument to gain for themselves more of the needed things of life.

Every candy maker knows that "terra alba," a white clay, is used in such proportions that it would shock the gum-chewers if they knew how much of that undigestible stuff wanders into the stomachs of the fair ladies. Throwing in sugar and other ingredients the candyworker is supposed to let the machines work the mixing to perfection, the worker tends the machine, he is supposed to see nothing when that "terra alba" is squeezed through the mixer.

Are the workers supposed to be the capitalists' keepers and help protect them against the effects of their quiet, legitimate business affairs? Terra alba may get into a heap of candy stuff in big chunks, unmixed. The workers turn that instrument against their own oppressors. They inform the candy eaters through a public notice that they have decided to turn the tables and use that sabotage for the gaining of their own ends instead of turning fraudulent profits in for their employers. The capitalists will know what it means for them, and they are growing frantic whenever they hear that there is an inclination on the part of workers to apply that weapon.

Every butcher workman knows he is expected to remain a meek, autonomous attachment to the job when working in and outside of the place of employment. But what they know about capitalist sabotage of meat products would fill volumes. Sinclair in his "Jungle" showed up, without exaggeration whatever, the extent to which capitalists and the meat barons order "sabotage," to use up every available piece of the animals, whether they be short-tailed and big, or long-tailed and small, running rampant in the store houses and the rooms where meat is converted into meat products. Armour and Swift never served notice on the soldiers in Cuba that embalmed beef would cause stomach trouble and even death. But in a "sabotage" campaign of butcher workmen in Vienna they served notice to the meat buyers of their intentions, that is, of using "sabotage" for their own good. So did packing house workers in Pittsburgh not hesitate to apply that method to gain their ends. In Vienna the owners of the shops found out to their discomfiture that meat sabotage worked better than a meat boycott. When the rodents instead of falling into the chopper and mixer to be ground up into pudding for Wiener Wurst, are hacked into large chunks and distributed in several sausages and meat products, the salesman will soon discover whether rat-legs, and rat-heads, unmixed and unassimilated to real pork meat, will pass inspection by the meat eaters. It's a horrible thing, this, but not more horrible than the sabotage for capitalist interests, when even the chopped-off fingers of workingmen are passed into the meat, as every workmen in the meat industry can testify to.

The whole list of adulterated foodstuffs proves only that the workers are supposed to do this "sabotage" without protest, for the interests of the exploiters. But as soon as they use the knowledge of these things to their own advantage it becomes a crime, an intrusion on the right of the employer to dictate absolutely what the employees must do when at his post of employment.

The hotel workers—cooks and waiters, the beer makers, the tobacco workers, could all tell about sabotage, and how in some stages of their contests for more rights they silently, by verbal agreement, would turn their own sabotage work in, in order to show the employers that they could use these things to their own advantage. Whether justifiable or not, it is being done. No amount of sophistry on the part of those who may be shocked to hear these things, will convince the workers that they are wrong in sometimes turning the tables against the capitalists.

SABOTAGE IMPLIES THE WITHDRAWAL OF EFFICIENCY FROM THE WORK.

The withdrawal of that efficiency to turn the fraud of capitalists into profits may run counter to the ethical standard of moralists, but it effects the most vulnerable part of the exploiters of labor, their pocket-book, and that's what the workers care for.

The withdrawal of the efficiency of the railroad service, by the railroad clerk misdirecting the loading bills and the freight handlers putting on wrong tags of destination on the cars, may cause a confusion hard to untangle, even partial paralyzation of systematic and orderly service and deliveries, but to the capitalists it has quite often brought home the lesson that, even if the worker is an attachment to the job, and is supposed to have no brain for himself, this withdrawal of that brain and efficiency is able to paralyze industries and prompt the employing class in making terms for the employee under which he again turns in his efficiency on the job he holds.

Each and every industry offers illustrations of capitalist sabotage, and presents suggestions how the withdrawal of efficiency, an indirect method, forces the capitalists to recognize labor's power in that direction. The common workers in the textile print shops withdraw their quickness to separate the aniline-soaked cloth from the piles. The employers, knowing that if the job is not done on a specified time thousands of dollars' worth of goods will go up in fire generated by the chemical decomposition of the colors, will rather accede to the demands of the workers than suffer incalculable loss.

The earlier day jurisdiction contests of the mine workers, the brewery workers, the packing house workers to have control over all workers in their respective industries, sprang originally from the conception that the direct action method of striking could more effectually be supplemented by the indirect method of sabotage. When the ice machine engineers in breweries, cold storage houses, packing houses, or hotels, withdraw from work, or only their efficiency to keep these machines running, for 24 hours or less, all the perishable goods have gone the natural road of decay. When the miners many times found that the strike brought no results, they knew that the withdrawal of engineers and pumpmen would work the sabotage with the aid of the waters flooding the mines.

Many a time workers lost by the "direct action" method, their strikes. They lost because the employers could secure strikebreakers to fill their places. But even in this machine age of production the efficiency of a worker is increased if he tends constantly to one job. It takes time for strikebreakers to acquire that efficiency, and then they are not there to look for that. Even after a lost strike most of the old workers are returned to their former positions, only their privileges on the job are curtailed. Then they decide not to turn out more work than did the strikebreakers during the strike, to withdraw their efficiency, do their duties as carelessly as the strikebreakers, and in ninety-nine out of a hundred cases they quickly obtained what by a strike they never could hope to get, the recognition of their rights to have something to say about the terms of employment.

Let it be conceded even, that sabotage action may run amuck. Nor will it be denied that often wanton destruction resulted, whenever it was applied by irresponsible individuals aggrieved. Going even further, let it be admitted that its use has been prostituted for anti-social purposes. But have not all other methods of the working class in the war against the oppressors been sometimes misused and wrongly applied?

We must above all investigate by whom sabotage is applied, and for what purposes. We must know the source of the abuses, and also its limitations. Then alone can an enlightened working class determine what must be done to stop the misuse of the weapons of the toilers in their struggles for better life conditions. Misuse is mostly done by those who strive only to discredit them, and to lay the blame for their own obscure actions at the door of those who declare, knowing that no matter how to achieve it, that the emancipation of the workers must be their own work, intelligently guided and directed.

MISUSE OF DIRECT AND INDIRECT METHODS.

If one is trained to consider the job a bargain-counter at which employer and employee meet on equal terms, for mutual bargaining, as the term used in the trade movement implies, he thereby binds himself not to impair the interests of his partner in the bargain during the period of the mutual understanding. Collectively the trades unionists are trained in that theory, and iron-clad contracts, looked upon as sacred instruments, prevent them from jeopardizing the interests of the employers during the life of such contracts. Belonging to a passing age they also believe in the law of competition. The competition on the bargain counter makes one craft unionist praise the virtues and qualification of his commodity, one craft, to the disadvantage of other crafts that may complete in the same line of business. "This competition between crafts for jurisdiction will in the long run give the award to the fittest, the most efficient," is the proclamation of Samuel Gompers before a convention of Stationary Firemen held in Washington, DC.

We will not talk here of the earlier functions and theories of trades unionism. Trades unions were useful agencies in by-gone days to use all the described methods, with no exception, to gain some control of shop conditions, thereby curtailing the economic power of the employing class. Today they function mostly to prevent the intelligent, class-conscious use of all these weapons, and serve even to allow groups of capitalists to misuse them in their competitive games against each other. The strike of trades unionists aims not to gain more control of the job conditions for all workers in a given plant or industry. The strike may be used to force non-members of employers' associations to either quit business or join the price combination of the employers, as in the case of the plumbers and horseshoers. The walk-out of one group of organized workers, or preferably of large numbers of unorganized toilers is used to gain slight concessions for other craftsmen in the same plant or industry with union contracts, to defeat the others, as it is done in most of the crafts in the textile, metal and other industries. The strike of workers in the same industry in one district is used to increase the prices of the commodity in other districts. Or a general strike, after serving months of notice on the employers, is arranged to sell the accumulated commodity at higher market prices, as so many suspensions of work in the coal mining industry have shown.

The boycott, through the union label, is used to boost the trade of one set of manufacturers without any consideration of the claims of all the workers in the same industry, and often to prevent the organization of men, women and children with lower wages and worse labor conditions, as it is done in the cigar industry, in the clothing-making, in the baking industry and others.

The destructive strike is applied to browbeat, to club, and even assassinate workers who are debarred by high initiation fees from these craft unions, or who are victims of the jurisdiction fights, the competition-struggle on the mutual bargain counter of capitalists and craft unionists.

In the political field the leaders of the craft union support the outrageous use of the governmental powers by openly boosting measures intended to protect the interests of employers or the capitalist class, thereby helping to increase the economic power of the latter, the absolute control of the job, as was done by the craft unionists in the steel and glass industries when they helped to boost the McKinley doctrine of high tariff. Or, by the conservative brotherhoods of railroad workers now supporting the railroad magnates in their claim that they would go bankrupt if the freight rates would be reduced. Or the United Mine Workers in agreeing with the coal operators in Illinois and other districts that they would abstain from supporting political measures intended to amend or improve existing mining laws for the protection of life and health of workers. There are too many instances to enumerate here, but even on the field of sabotage the capitalists have taken care that the trades unions safeguard them against any injuries from that direction. In contracts with the mine workers' unions it is directly stipulated that the United Mine Workers, the organization of employees, will not permit the damaging of property by water, as result of engineers leaving their positions. They agree to fill the places of any who would eventually quit with such an object in view. When, as in Danville, Ill., district in 1910, the striking miners try to make the pumpmen and engineers withdraw their work, the officials support the mine owners in their clamor for the militia to stop such attempts. To prevent the work of "sabotage," in its natural course, the striking brewery workers of Los Angeles make provisions that the ice machines be not stopped so that the warm temperature in the cellar might not sabotage the immense amount of fluid. The capitalists only too well know how this instrument has impeded their absolute power over the worker's job, and may do so again. The trades union contract gives them, what will in their opinion be the best safeguard against the application of sabotage.

So even mass movements of workers for the exercise of their power by direct or indirect actions are utilized for anti-social purposes, by agencies that the capitalists time and again have used to prevent a concerted move of the entire working class to undermine the foundation of the economic and political power of their oppressors.

CLASS ORGANIZATION, CLASS ACTION.

The working people economically and politically united as a class will be the agency, and the only organ of human efforts by which the proper use of all the instruments of direct and indirect action will be wielded for the protection of the interests of the human forces, who as producers, are the source of economic power of those who hold them to their bondage.

Class unity implies organization. But such an organization must be based on the knowledge what class unity and class action means. In many matters the capitalists may often be divided; on their monopoly over the job of the workers, their collective producing power, they are united, and form a class for themselves. We have shown in the beginning that the land, the factories, the machines, the railroads, the steamships, etc., in themselves yield no economic power to their owners. Only the human labor used in their operation constitutes that power. Any infringement on that domain of power, even in the slightest degree, is an intrusion on the monopoly that the capitalists possess. Only a little evident break in that foundation endangers the whole structure upon which present day society is pivoted. For the protection of that dam which keeps the stored-up energies of the whole world harnessed for production for profit, they put out their guardsmen, their courts, their labor lieutenants, their reform fakirs, their law makers, their law executors, their police powers, their soldiers, militia, etc.

The pressure against that construction may ofttimes become so strong that its very safety is endangered. The capitalists, then, rather tap the enormous reservoir and let surplus energies go to waste before they concede the use of these economic, resources for other than the creation of profits.

The monopoly of the jobs is their stronghold. That alone must be undermined, attacked and completely destroyed ultimately, if ever the working class wishes to see its economic and political freedom established. This is the direct point at which working-class activity must always aim, regardless of the methods that may be employed to successfully accomplish the task.

But are these guardians of that economic structure to be brushed aside with a wishbone so that the mines may be laid for the removal of that dam? Are these protective agencies not in strength corresponding to the power of those who hold the monopoly over the places of work, and thereby also over the destinies of the producers? And is not the strongest weapon of the capitalist class, their best guardsmen on the line, the ignorance of the millions of workers who still cling to the idea that it is a God-ordained privilege that gives a few the right to hold this monopoly over the opportunities of the many? Is it not that great mass that is supporting the employing class in guarding their supremacy over the workers' life conditions, thereby allowing them to wield that economic power based on the monopoly of the jobs that the workers must have in order to live?

Those of the working class who have analyzed the social system from all angles know that it would be ridiculous to attack the system with only one instrument. They will scorn the idea that they should ignore the others, which the capitalists will in turn use to defeat the efforts of the workers to aim directly at the foundation of the system.

Therefore, the workers must use all actions possible to advance against the citadel of the employing class.

POLITICAL RIGHTS ESSENTIAL.

Political rights must be secured and safeguarded. The right of free speech, of a free unmuzzled press, of undisturbed assemblage are prerequisite for the formation and maintenance of class organizations of workers. When they are denied direct action is applied to secure them. And the more severe the measures are by which the workers are to be debarred from enjoying these privileges, the more pronounced will the efforts be to get out of the stage where violent and even destructive actions are needed to show that the desire of the producers to get access to the source of economic power can never be stopped by repressions. Only where the conditions exist, or are established, that the guarantee of political rights assure the preparation for class action through class organizations of workers, will the struggle for the control of the job be void of the features that are denounced by the average man, because human life, the life of working people, is often placed in jeopardy in the struggle for more rights. The aim of political, indirect action of the working class tends primarily to remove the guardian of that structure behind which the immense producing energies are harnessed and stored up for capitalist production. By an agitation, protected by political rights previously secured, such as for instance anti-militaristic propaganda, it is endeavored to weaken the fortifications of the structure. With soldiers standing with the muzzle of their guns turned to the ground the attack on the main fortress of capitalism can be easier accomplished. With the law-making and law-executing agencies of capitalism, as guardians of capitalist interests, out of the way, the foundation may be easier undermined. It must even be conceded that political parties, exercising the mandates of the working class, may be able to remove the most pernicious opponents to the rights of the producers to the jobs and all the proceeds of that job, and place in their stead advocates of working-class interests. But then, this should never divert the activities of the workers from aiming constantly and directly at the foundation of all these agencies, the economic power of the oppressors and exploiters. A political party claiming to represent the toilers may have its functionaries in the lawmaking and law-executing agencies. But it should be for the purpose alone to facilitate the formation of class organization of workers for the attack against the seat of capitalist power, to wit: the monopoly over the places of employment. A political party, no matter what good the intentions of its constituency may be, by the nature of its composition, cannot be a class organization of workers. It can use but one method in battling for its objects and aims, the lawmaking and law-executing agencies of capitalism. It has but one road upon which it ought to pursue its course for the realization of its claims and aims, the road of education. If this education, though, is not based on the actual conditions in the social system, it is worse than useless, it is confusing and destructive.

CLASS ORGANIZATION—INDUSTRIAL UNION.

The class organization of the workers for class action on all lines must therefore be a combination that brings together all the men, the women and the children who are furnishing today the economic power to the exploiters of labor. It must embrace all those who give value to all industrial resources of the world, by their producing power being applied to the instruments of production and exchange. It must be a union of toilers whose object must be to undermine the source of industrial power wielded today by the exploiters of human labor power. It must be an organization which teaches the fundamental principles of industrial solidarity of all workers so to break and to destroy the monopoly of the capitalist class over the jobs. It must be an industrial union, uniting therein the working people for direct and indirect actions in the workshops and against the political outposts of capitalism. It must struggle to the end that the results of the collective labor of the working class may gradually accrue in larger measure to the producers, and that finally the jobs of the world's workshops be controlled absolutely by those who give value to and create wealth with the enormous instruments and agencies of production. It must, by virtue of its class character, protect itself against the misapplication of actions for the support of foul designs of the employing class by recognizing the irrepressible antagonism of interests between the workers and the shirkers. It must combine the interests of the workers so strongly together that all actions, all methods of attacks, will be dictated by the mandates of the workers as a class, so that the irresponsible acts of individuals and the reactionary methods of craft unionism be discarded and made obsolete as a means of warfare.

SOLIDARITY OF LABOR STRONGER THAN VIOLENCE.

Thus organized, the working class would need not fear the misuse of its own political or economic power by the employing class. Violence, destruction of life would be needless and useless. On the path to the industrial and political freedom of the toilers there will be many more skirmishes. But will it not be better, when, for example, street car employees are compelled to strike all together, none tied down by contracts, and moved only, by the feeling that the injury done to one is the injury to all, would quit—the power house workers, the switch tenders, electricians etc., united with the others? There would be no need of overturning cars, of beating up alleged strikebreakers or non-union brothers and the use of destructive means to show that there is an industrial revolt on. With their arms folded the workers would know that the power-houses could not furnish the required power, and the whole system must stand still. No violence needed to stop operation, when all quit at once. Withdrawal of labor power from the places of employment, or the removal of efficiency (sabotage) would then be organized class expression. Would it not be better to let the mines fill with water when engineers and pumpmen and all the rest quit together, than to have human life destroyed when, as often it has been, the striking miners try to gain their objects by an attack on those who under contract today continue to slave under the protection of sheriffs and troops, while their brethren are being bled to death, in an unequal struggle with their oppressors? What is more worth, the welfare of the workers or the hundreds of thousands of dollars of beef stored up in the packing houses? What then is wrong when the shutting down of ice machines either tends to destroy all the stored UP wealth, or the employers are forced to give more of the means of existence, so that hungry, starving children may be better nourished, and the daughters of the toilers be protected against falling into the gutter of life?

All the resolutions of condemnation and protest, either dictated by ignorance or actuated by a desire to serve the interests of the capitalists, will not restrain the workers from weighing every measure that they conceive to be good in their efforts to get a larger, and finally complete control of that source of economic power, the place of production. The more they learn to know where their power lies the more will they strive and battle for the amelioration of their present day conditions. They will fight for better wages, shorter hours of work, more rights, for the undermining of the power of the employer. They will organize as a class for class action on all fields of activity. They are doing it now, until the day will come, must come, when the structure of capitalism will fall by the pressure of the attacking forces, and the energies of the world's workers will no longer be used to grind profits for a few parasites. With the structure in collapse, will be swept aside also the force of political guardians of capitalist interests, and a new reconstructed society, based on the control of the powers of production by the producers, will assure to the inhabitants of the world that peace, that pursuit of happiness, that plentifulness in material and intellectual requirements needed to establish the perfect, harmonious co-operation of all members of society for a most harmonious and beautiful life on earth for all who live.

The solidarity of labor for such accomplishment must be organized today in class organizations, for class action. Such are the Industrial Workers of the World.

For information write to:
INDUSTRIAL WORKERS OF THE WORLD
518 Cambridge Building,
160 Fifth Avenue, Chicago, Illinois

SABOTAGE

ITS HISTORY, PHILOSOPHY & FUNCTION

WALKER C. SMITH

John Farmer's First Lesson

Solidarity, September 2, 1916

Cartoon by Ralph Chaplin for the IWW's
Agricultural Workers' Organization (1916)

Silent Agitator Sticker
by Ralph Chaplin (circa 1916)

Sabotage
Its History, Philosophy & Function
Walker C. Smith

FOREWORD

This little work is the essence of all available material collected on the subject of Sabotage for a period of more than two years. Thanks are due to the many rebels who gave assistance, and especially to Albin Braida, who made for me what I think to be the first. English translation of Pouget's work on Sabotage. From this last pamphlet extracts have been taken and adaptations made to suit American conditions.

The object of this work is to awaken the producers to a consciousness of their industrial power. It is dedicated, not to those who advocate but to those who use sabotage.

—Walker C. Smith.

I

NO THEORY, NO PHILOSOPHY, NO LINE OF ACTION IS SO GOOD as claimed by its advocates nor so bad as painted by its critics. Sabotage is no exception to this rule. Sabotage according to the

capitalists and the political socialists, is synonymous with murder, rapine, arson, theft; is illogical, vile, unethical, reactionary,
destructive of society itself. To many anarchist theorists it is the
main weapon of industrial warfare, overshadowing mass solidarity, industrial formation and disciplined action. Some even go so
far as to claim that sabotage can usher in the new social order.
Somewhere between these two extreme views can be found the
truth about sabotage.

Three versions are given of the source of the word. The one
best known is that a striking French weaver cast his wooden
shoe—called a sabot—into the delicate mechanism of the loom
upon leaving the mill. The confusion that resulted, acting to the
workers' benefit, brought to the front a line of tactics that took
the name of SABOTAGE. Slow work is also said to be at the basis
of the word, the idea being that wooden shoes are clumsy and so
prevent quick action on the part of the workers. The third idea is
that Sabotage is coined from the slang term that means "putting
the boots" to the employers by striking directly at their profits
without leaving the job. The derivation, however, is unimportant.
It is the thing itself that causes commotion among employers and
politicians alike. What then is Sabotage?

Sabotage is the destruction of profits to gain a definite, revolutionary, economic end. It has many forms. It may mean the
damaging of raw materials destined for a scab factory or shop.
It may mean the spoiling of a finished product. It may mean the
displacement of parts of machinery or the disarrangement of a
whole machine where that machine is the one upon which the
other machines are dependent for material. It may mean working
slow. It may mean poor work. It may mean missending packages,
giving overweight to customers, pointing out defects in goods, using the best of materials where the employer desires adulteration
and also the telling of trade secrets. In fact, it has as many varia-
tions as there are different lines of work.

Note this important point, however. **Sabotage does not seek
nor desire to take human life.** Neither is it directed against the

consumer except where wide publicity has been given to the fact that the sabotaged product is under the ban. **A boycotted product is at all times a fit subject for sabotage.** The aim is to hit the employer in his vital spot, his heart and soul, in other words, his pocketbook. The consumer is struck only when he interposes himself' between the two combatants.

On the other hand, sabotage is simply one of the many weapons in labor's arsenal. It is by no means the greatest one. Solidaric action is mightier than the courageous acts of a few. Industrial class formation gives a strength not to be obtained by mere tactics. Self discipline and co-operative action are necessary if we are to build a new social order as well as destroy the old. Sabotage is merely a means to an end; a means that under certain conditions might be dispensed with and the end still be gained.

Sabotage will sometimes be misused, flagrantly so; the same is true of every one of the weapons of labor. The main concern to revolutionists is whether the use of sabotage will destroy the power of the masters in such a manner as to give the workers a greater measure of industrial control. On that point depends its usefulness to the working class.

II

Sabotage is not a form of action brought forth from French conditions. It dates back to the earliest days of human exploitation. It is born of class struggles—of man's inhumanity to man. From serfdom to wage slavery the enslaved class has instinctively tried to render less to the master than was expected of it. This unconscious sabotage shows the irreconcilable antagonism between capitalist and laborer—master and slave.

Sabotage was not formally baptized as a word to describe a formula of social struggle until the Confederal Congress of Tolosa in 1897. Open advocacy of the idea and conscious sabotage in place of instinctive action began in France about this time. It had been preached in England and Scotland for many years before that under the name of "Ca' Canny." This phrase of Scotch origin meant "Go slow," or to be more literal, "Don't hurry up." From a publication "The Social Museum" an instance is gained of the use of sabotage by the Scotch.

"In 1889 the organized dockers of Glasgow demanded a ten per cent increase of wages but met with the refusal of the employers. Strike breakers were brought in from among the agricultural laborers and the dockers had to acknowledge defeat and return to work on the old, wage scale. But before the men resumed their work, their secretary of the union delivered to them the following address:

"You are going back to work at the old wage. The employers have repeated time and time again that they were delighted with the work of the agricultural laborers who had taken our places for several weeks during the strike. But we have seen them at work; we have seen that they could not even walk a vessel, that they dropped half of the merchandise they carried, in short, that two of them could hardly do the work of one of us. Nevertheless, the employers have declared themselves enchanted by the work of these fellows; well, then, there is nothing left for us but do the same and to practice Ca' Canny. Work as the agricultural laborers worked. Only they often fell into the water; it is useless for you to do the same."

"This order was obeyed to the letter. After a few days the contractors sent for the general secretary of the dockers and begged him to tell the dockers to work as before and that they were ready to grant the ten per cent increase."

Balzac, writing three-quarters of a century ago, gave a good illustration of sabotage in describing the bloody uprising of Lyons in 1831.

"There have been many things said about the uprising of Lyons, of the republic cannonaded in the streets, but no one has told the truth. The republic seized the movement as an insurgent seizes a rifle.

"The commerce of Lyons is a commerce without courage; as soon as an ounce of silk is manufactured it is asked for and payment made at once. When the demand stops, the workers are dying of starvation; when they are working they earn barely enough to live upon. The prisoners are more happy than they.

"After the July revolution misery reached the point where the workers were compelled to raise a standard: 'Bread or Death!'—a standard which the government should have considered.

"The republicans had felt out the revolt and they organized the spinners who fought in double shifts. Lyons had its three days. Then everything became normal again and the poor went back to their dog kennels.

"The spinners who had, until then, transformed into useful goods the silk which was weighed to them in cocoons, laid aside probity. They began to grease their fingers with oil. With scrupulous ability they rendered the correct weight, but the silks were all specked with oil. The commerce of the silk manufactures was infested with greasy goods which caused a loss to Lyons and to a portion of the French commerce."

This action, as Balzac points out, was nothing more than the workers taking revenge for having been the victims of bayonets when they had asked for bread. But sabotage is something more than simply the equivalent of an oppression received; it has an economic foundation.

III

There exists today a labor market in which the wage workers sell their power to perform various task asked of them by the purchasers—the employing class. The labor power of the workers is a commodity. In selling their merchandise the workers must sell themselves along with it. Therefore they are slaves—wage slaves. In purchasing goods from a merchant one receives an inferior quality for a low price. For a low price—poor products. If this applies to hats and shoes, why not equally to the commodity sold by the laborer? It is from this reasoning that there arises the idea: **For poor wages—bad work.** This thought is a natural one even to those who agree with society as it is now constituted. To those who do not look upon the wage system as a finality and who have come to regard the employers in their true light—as thieves of the laborers' product—the idea of sabotage commends itself still more strongly. It is a logical weapon for the revolutionist.

Economists have shown that the wages of the workers are not determined by their product. Wages are simply the market price of the commodity called **labor power**. Wages are not raised or lowered as the productivity of the worker ebbs and flows. They are conditioned upon the supply and demand, the standard of living where the wages are paid, and the relative strength of the organizations of workers and employers. Not many wage workers have studied the deeper economists, but the ditch digger knows that when he has finished the ditch upon which he is at work he must hunt another master. He instinctively slows up. Self-preservation is one of the first laws of nature. His action has value from a class standpoint, for either more ditch diggers must be employed to complete the work within a given time, or else there is less competition in the labor market for those extra days he labors.

Many who condemn sabotage will be found to be unconscious advocates of it. Think of the absurd position of the "craft union socialists" who decry sabotage and, in almost the same breath, condemn the various efficiency systems of the employers! By opposing "scientific management" they are doing to potential profits what the saboteurs are doing to actual profits. The one prevents efficiency, the other withdraws it. Incidentally it might be said that sabotage is the only effective method of warding off the deterioration of the worker that is sure to follow the performance of the same monotonous task minute after minute, day in and day out. Sabotage also offers the best method to combat the evil known as "speeding up." None but the workers know how great this evil is. It is one of the methods by which employers coin wealth from death, consuming the very lives of the toilers. By payment of slightly higher wage to the stronger and more dexterous slave, the rest are forced to keep pace. Those who fall by the way are unceremoniously cast aside to beg, steal or starve. One method used by the saboteur to stop this form of scabbery is illustrated by the following occurrence:

Building laborers were wheeling barrows of material to an electric hoist, following the rate of speed set by their higher paid taskmaster. The pace became so swift that those who were weaker could no longer keep up. During the noon hour one of the men stepped to the wheel barrow of the speeder and tightened the burrs on the wheel. Upon resuming work the task master started at his usual pace but soon was obliged to slow down through sheer weariness. No class-conscious worker will join the moralists and vote catchers in condemning this action.

In the steel mills the speeding up process has become so distressing to the average worker that still greater steps are taken for self-protection. In fact, in speaking of these class traitors, it is often remarked that "Something dropped on their foot often affects their head." There are many points of similarity between the speeder and the favored steer in the stock yards who is trained to lead the other steers into the killing pens.

England offers an example of a practical method of limiting the output. Due to effective, widespread, systematic sabotage the brick masons there lay as a day's work, less than one-third the number of brick required from their brother craftsmen in America. Any reduction in pay is met with a counter reduction in the work. Sabotage means, therefore, that the workers directly fight the conditions imposed by the masters in accordance with the formula "Poor wages—bad work."

IV

Actions which might be classed as "capitalist sabotage" are used by the different exploiting and professional classes. The truck farmer packs his largest fruits and vegetables on top. The merchant sells inferior articles as "something just as good." The doctor gives "bread-pills" or other harmless concoctions in cases where the symptoms are puzzling. The builder uses poorer material than demanded in the specifications. The manufacturer adulterates foodstuffs and clothing. All these are for the purpose of gaining more profits. Carloads of potatoes were destroyed in Illinois recently; cotton was burned in the Southern states; coffee was destroyed by the Brazilian planters; barge loads of onions were dumped overboard in California; apples are left to rot on the trees of whole orchards in Washington; and hundreds of tons of foodstuffs are held in cold storage until rendered unfit for consumption. All to raise prices. Yet it is exploiters of this character who are loudest in condemnation of sabotage when it is used to benefit the workers.

Some forms of capitalist sabotage are legalized, others are not. But whether or not the various practices are sanctioned by law, it is evident that they are more harmful to society as a whole than is the sabotage of the workers. Capitalists cause imperfect dams to be constructed, and devastating floods sweep whole sections of the country. They have faulty bridges erected, and wrecks cause great loss of life. They sell steamer tickets, promising absolute security, and sabotage the life-saving equipment to the point where hundreds are murdered, as witness the Titanic. The General Slocum disaster in an example of capitalist sabotage on the life preservers, The Iroquois Theater fire is an example of sabotage by exploiters who assured the public that the fire curtain was made of asbestos. There are also the Primero, the Drakesboro, the Cherry mine disasters and the terrible Triangle Shirtwaist tragedy. The cases could be multiplied indefinitely. These capitalist murderers constitute themselves the mentors of the morals of those slaves who "have nothing to lose but their chains." Only fools will take their ethics from such knaves. **Capitalist opposition to sabotage is one of its highest recommendations.**

Capitalist sabotage aims to benefit a small group of non-producers, while working-class sabotage seeks to help the whole body of producers at the expense of the parasites. The frank position of the class-conscious worker is that capitalist sabotage is **wrong** because it harms the workers; working-class sabotage is right because it aids the workers. This view comes from the position the proletarians occupy in the class war. A word about that class war.

To the rebellious toiler the class war is no mere theory. It is a grim realty. To him it is not a polite sparring match according to Marquis of Queensbury rules with four years between each round. It is love of liberty, and war against the exploiters. "All's fair in love and war."

Because the revolutionist has discarded the moral code of the master class and has spit in the face of bourgeois ethics, it does not necessarily follow that there is no rule regulating his conduct. He is, in fact, so strongly actuated by an ideal that he has left the arena of words to enter the realm of action. **Sabotage is a direct application of the idea that property has no rights that its creators are bound to respect.** Especially is this true when the creators of the wealth of the world are in hunger and want amid the abundance they have produced, while the idle few have all the good things of life.

However secret must be sabotage, when used by the individual instead of the whole body, it is taking its place in the rising moral code of the property less toilers just in proportion as it is being openly advocated. The outspoken propaganda of sabotage and its widespread use are true reflections of economic conditions. The current ethical code, with all existing laws and institutions, is based upon private property in production. **Why expect those who have no stake in society, as it is now constituted, to continue to contribute to its support?**

V

The charge that sabotage is "immoral," "unethical," "uncivilized," and the like, does not worry the rebellious workers so long as it is effective in inflicting injury to the employers' profits. As it aids the workers in their fight it will find increasing favor in their eyes. In war the strategic move is to cut off the opposing force from its base of supplies. Sabotage seeks to curtail profits and in conjunction with other weapons to abolish finally the surplus value, or unpaid labor, that is the source of the employers' power.

"You are immoral" cry employers and politicians alike. Our answer is that all morals today are based upon private property. Even so-called sexual immorality is condemned while universally practiced, because it violates the principle of inheritance in property and is in defiance of customs generally accepted but seldom inquired into. When the workers accept their morals from the capitalist class they are in a sorry way indeed. **The question is not, Is sabotage immoral?—but, Does sabotage get the goods?**

"You are destroying civilization" is likewise hurled against us, to which we reply in the language of the street: "We should worry!" **Civilization is a lie. A civilization that is builded upon the bended backs of toiling babes; a civilization that is reared upon the sweating, starving, struggling mass of mankind; a civilization whose 'very existence depends upon a constant army of hungry, servile and law-abiding unemployed, is scarcely worthy of consideration at the hands of those whom it has so brutally outraged. The saboteur carries on his work in order to hasten the day of working-class victory, when for the first time in human history we shall have a civilization that is worthy of the name.**

What is more civilized than for the workers to create powder that refuses to explode?'

What is more civilized than to work slow and thus force employers to give a living to more of the unemployed?

What is more civilized than to spike the guns when they are trained on our working-class brothers in other countries?

What is more civilized than to waste the adulterations given the workers to place in food, thus making it unprofitable, to sell impure products?

Sabotage will civilize the soldier, the militiaman, the police, the speeder, the slave driver, the food poisoner, the shoddy manufacturer, the profit grabber of high and low degree, and even the politician.

Those who oppose sabotage on ethical grounds are supporters of capitalist theft and are faithful watchdogs of the strong boxes wherein the masters store stolen wealth. Revolutionists have no time to waste in taking lessons in correct manners from those who do no useful labor in society. In advocating sabotage we hope to show that the workers should rid their minds of the last remnant of bourgeois cant and hypocrisy and by its use develop courage and individual

From sabotage to gain better conditions it is a logical step to direct sabotage against the repressive and perverting forces of capitalism.

VI

The press is one of the greatest agencies used by the employers to keep the workers in subjection. It is dominated by the industrial masters. Sometimes the press is owned directly, sometimes through a mortgage or a secured loan. More often, the subsidization of the press is accomplished through advertising patronage. But at all times the power of the capitalist press depends upon the servility of the slaves who do all the work of setting up, printing and distributing the lies of the masters. Sabotage is the most effective weapon for the stopping of newspaper attacks upon the workers and their organizations.

As a whole the reporters are favorable to the workers. They have to follow the policy of the papers to hold their jobs, however. They can use sabotage on the masters by their handling of the news. The editors of the various departments will color the matter anyhow, in accordance with wishes of advertisers or stockholders of the paper. But when an article is written that is harmful to the working class there are many ways in which it can be saboted. The linotype operator can misplace a portion of the copy. The proofreader can insert or remove the word "not" and thus change a knock to a boost. The make-up man can place another article where it was intended the lie should go or he can insert a part of another article under the offending heading so that it will apparently read correctly and yet will not contain the harmful material, The stereotyper can damage the face of the, offending article so that it will not print. These are but a few of the many methods that might be used. All of these "accidents" are happening every day in publishing plants and it but remains to direct them to a revolutionary end. With more class consciousness along these lines the employers will find it does not pay to lie about the workers.

One of the repressive forces of capitalism, the militia, can be made useless by the extension of the use of sabotage. One saboteur can make harmless toys of the entire equipment of a company. When a trainload of soldiers are dispatched to a strike scene, where they always act in the interest of the employers, the train can be saboted. In Parma, Italy, for example, the farm laborers struck. Soldiers were ordered to the scene. The engineers refused to pull the train from the depot. Volunteers to man the engines were secured from the ranks of the soldiers. When these scabs entered the cab they found that some vital part of each engine had been misplaced. They were forced to walk to Parma. Bridges disappeared in advance of the line of march. When the weary and disgusted troops arrived at the scene of the agricultural strike they found that the strikers had won and were back at work.

Realizing that the railroads are the arteries of commerce the capitalists of this country have practically purchased the engineers by a high wage and the establishment of an aristocracy of labor. But a few rebels are bound to creep into their ranks. Even if every one of them remained a traitor to the workers by being loyal to the employers still they could not escape sabotage. A bar of soap in the boiler would keep the soldiers at home or else force them to march to the strike. If this were not possible, there are water tanks where the tender must be filled and the saboteur can "Let the Gold Dust Twins do the work."

In case of wars, which every intelligent worker knows are wholesale murders of workers to enrich the master class, there is no weapon so forceful to defeat the employers as sabotage by the rebellious workers in the two warring countries. **Sabotage will put a stop to war when resolutions, parliamentary appeals and even a call for general refusal to serve are impotent.** But, as stated before sabotage is but one phase of the question. Anti-military and anti-patriotic agitation must also carried on.

Sabotage is a mighty force as a revolutionary tactic against the repressive forces of capitalism, whether those repressions be direct or through the State.

VII

"It is guerilla warfare," is another cry against sabotage. Well, what of it? Has not guerilla warfare proven itself to be a useful thing to repel invaders and to make gains for one or the other of the opposing forces? Do not the capitalists use guerilla warfare? Guerilla warfare brings out the courage of individuals, it develops initiative, daring, resoluteness and audacity. Sabotage does the same for its users. It is to the social war what guerillas are to national wars. If it does no more than awaken a portion of the workers from their lethargy it will have been justified. But it will do more than that; it will keep the workers awake and will incite them to do battle with masters. It will give added hope to the militant minority, the few who always bear the brunt of the struggle.

The saboteur is the sharpshooter of the revolution. He has the courage and the daring to invade the enemy's country in the uniform of a "loyal," that is to say—subservient, worker. **But he knows that loyalty to the employer means treason to his class.** Sabotage is the smokeless powder of the social war. It scores a hit, while its source is seldom detected. It is so universally feared by the employers that they do not even desire that it be condemned for fear slave class may learn still more its great value.

Indeed, it can be seen that the masters are powerless in the face of this weapon. In the realm of production the masters do not enter except by indirection. The creation of wealth is the work of the wage slave class, and every tendency of this class is toward sabotage.

The time clock has come as sign that the boss recognizes the instinctive sabotage that is universal. In many establishments there is even a time clock in front of each toilet, with a time limit for the toilers to remain inside. But where is there a factory that has not its saboteurs who show their class solidarity by ringing in time for some of their fellow workers? In many establishments the time clock has an unaccountable habit of getting out of order and so costing the firm more than the amount of labor time saved otherwise. As a check against the spread of sabotage the employers have their paid writers to tell tales of how success in life is sure to attend the worker who does not watch the clock and who endeavors at every opportunity to save money for the employer. But there are more of the workers who are coming to see that any saving that is made is not reflected in their pay envelope, but simply means larger profits to those who are already getting the bulk of the good things of life. They also know that where one might possibly forge ahead by being a "boss-lover," the same line of action on the part of the whole force would reduce the number of employees needed and probably result in their dismissal. Knowing this they are scornful of Elbert Hubbard's veiled preachments against sabotage.

Those who denounce sabotage as "unfair" are also seen to be supporters of the kind of unions that notify the employers six months in advance of a strike, thus allowing them to procure scabs or to stock-pile so as to have material with which to supply the demand for goods while the workers are starving. The same moralists also hold that it is wrong for the miners to call out the pumpman on strike because the mines would flood, ignoring the fact that such action would quickly bring the employer to terms.

VIII

In warfare a flank movement is always feared by each of the opposing forces. In the social war sabotage is the best kind of a flank movement upon our enemy the employing class. An actual instance will serve to illustrate the point.

On an orchard farm in the state of Washington a disagreement arose over conditions on the job. A strike took place. The I.W.W. members among the strikes immediately telephoned to the union in the nearest city. When the employer arrived in town looking for a new crew he was rather surprised at his speedy success. Full fare was paid for the men and the railway train was boarded. At the first stop, about two miles from the city, the whole crew deserted the train. They were all members of the union. Returning to the city the farmer picked up a second crew. He arranged to have them pay their own fare, same to be refunded upon their arrival on the farm. This crew went through all right and worked for a while under the farmer's direction. Thinking the strike was successfully broken the employer finally busied himself with other matters for the rest of the day. Next morning upon visiting the work the farmer was surprised to find that 1,000 young trees had been planted upside down, their roots waving to the breeze as mute evidence of solidarity and sabotage. No further argument was needed to convince the farmer of the "justice" of the demands of the original crew.

This instance also shows that sabotage is not always an individual tactic. It ofttimes develops into mass action. Slowing up on the job is the most frequent form of mass sabotage, but a commonly related incident shows one of its other forms.

A gang of section men working on a railroad in Indiana were notified of a cut in their wages. The workers immediately took their shovels to the blacksmith shop and cut two inches from the scoops. Returning to the work they told the boss: "Short pay, short shovels."

Every cut in wages is met by a decrease in efficiency on the part of the workers. It remains for the militants to show that mass sabotage can be used to counteract the decreased wages that do not appear in terms of money but arise from the higher cost of living. When this is plain to the workers it will be only a step for them to use sabotage as lever by which to raise wages and, in the hands of the most rebellious, as a means to destroy profits utterly. For the piece workers other methods of sabotage must be used. They, naturally enough, are not interested in diminishing their product. Sabotage can be used in the quality or upon the materials and tools. It is useless to try to give all the different methods that are capable of being used. Each line of work dictates its own methods.

The one point must ever be borne in mind, however, that sabotage is not directed toward the consumer. The reason for sabotage is to strike a blow at the employing class profits and that is the thing that must always be uppermost in the mind of the saboteur. But take a theatre strike, where the patrons are fully aware that a boycott is on and the consumer—the playgoer—is then considered an ally of the employer and therefore to be treated as an enemy. The motion picture operators, especially in Chicago, have used sabotage to good advantage to clear the houses of unfair patrons. They simply dropped some vile smelling chemicals upon the floor during the performance and then made a quiet and speedy exit. The audience generally followed the example within a short time. This method was used only after an extensive boycott of the theatre in question had been advertised.

It is quite natural that the employing class try to have it generally understood that sabotage means poisoning soup, putting ground glass in bread, dynamiting buildings and the like, so the revolutionists must at all times emphasize the point that **sabotage is not aimed at the consumer but at the heart and soul of the employing class—the pocketbook.**

IX

"It will be met by the lockout," is another argument advanced against the use of sabotage. That is to say, the employer, finding sabotage in use in his factory, will cut off all of his profits in order to try to save a portion of them! But let a lockout be used and will not wage workers have to be employed as soon as operations are resumed? Will not the employer have to hire the same saboteurs, who have remained unknown to him? If workers are imported, cannot saboteurs get on the job in the guise of scabs?

A little thought on the subject shows that a lockout is impracticable in the face of sabotage. No employer locks out his force with the intention of keeping them out permanently. The workers must be re-employed. Their lockout experiences will drive home the class struggle more than would a thousand lectures on the subject, and many of them will return to work, as was predicted in the Lawrence strike, "with bitterness in their hearts and emery dust in their pockets." The employers, however, resort to the lockout only when all else has failed. Even when using this weapon they seek to have it appear as a strike, and they launch it at a time favorable to themselves in every particular, and therefore unfavorable to the workers. They hope, by such a lockout, to cause the workers to lose faith in the strike as a weapon; failing to note the fact that workers strike because they must, and not through mere desire. **They do not know that no agitator can cause a strike, no writer can call sabotage into use, no social revolution can be created and consummated, unless all the socially necessary elements of discontent are present.**

The direct lockout, even when it serves the immediate end of the employers, is harmful to their class interests as a whole. Even Gompers would scarcely dare preach "mutual interests" to locked out workers. Instead of blaming themselves for having struck, or placing the blame upon inefficient strike leadership, all the hatred of the workers is directed against the employers. **Armed with a knowledge of sabotage the workers return to their task, more terrible in defeat than in victory.**

Nor can the military forces be successfully employed against sabotage. The employers could not long afford to have a soldier to guard each worker. The workers, in fact, would immediately rebel when placed under such espionage. Neither is there any surety that sabotage will not have permeated the army. It is there already and it is growing in favor. Even were the workers to allow the military rule it might mean that sabotage would cease for the time being, to break out all the more fiercely the moment the soldiers were withdrawn, but more likely the natural resentment against such espionage would lead to an increased amount of sabotage. Wealth cannot be created with bayonets. The employers well know that their rule rests upon the peaceful acquiescence of the workers. They will scarcely undermine their own foundation by employing soldiers to massacre an entire force when a militant minority use sabotage.

Now that the capitalist class are ceasing even to perform the slight task of nominal superintendence in the industries to which they hold legal title, they are entitled to absolutely no consideration at the hands of the actual producers of wealth. Their withdrawal also means that the slight remaining cheek to sabotage is being removed. Eliminating all the obviously master class objections there remain but two pertinent questions from the point of view of the class-conscious wage worker. Does sabotage destroy working-class solidarity? Will sabotage continue to disarrange industry when the workers have taken possession?

Taking up the two questions in turn it can be shown that sabotage is not a boomerang that will return to slay those who use it.

X

Working-class solidarity is simply the result of a consciousness of power. Sabotage, by arming the workers with a weapon which the masters cannot wrest from them adds greatly to the feeling of strength.

Mass sabotage is in itself a sign of solidarity. The concerted withdrawal of efficiency, by slowing down or other means, is sure to bind the workers closer together. This is true whether they are organized or not. In case they are organized it gives to the workers a greater sense of security as well as additional industrial control.

Individual acts of sabotage, performed to the end that class benefit be derived, can in no way militate against solidarity. Rather they promote unity. The saboteur involves no one but himself and is impelled to take the risk by reason of his strong class desires.

Solidarity between the capitalists does not seem to be affected by their use of sabotage. That they fight each other with that potent weapon is quite evident. That they use it upon the workers is also easily seen. But nowhere can it be shown that there has been a division in the ranks of their fighting organizations, when the workers were doing battle against them, as a result of their use of sabotage.

Various cases of this capitalist sabotage might be quoted. Competitors of the Standard Oil Company often found that legal documents had been improperly executed for them. Rivals of the Sugar Trust had foreign materials introduced into their shipments, and in the fight of Havemeyer against Spreckels the latter's machinery had an unaccountable habit of getting out of order. A Denver brewing company almost ruined a competitor by hiring men to spread the story that a decomposed body had been found at the bottom of its rival's brew-vat. But when it comes to robbing the wage workers these capitalist saboteurs are "banded together like thieves at a fair."

Several of the so-called "muck-raking" magazines have been forced to suspend through the use of sabotage. Hampton's was killed in that manner by those capitalists who saw their interests menaced. The Appeal to Reason has been a sufferer at the hands of capitalist saboteurs who pied their mailing lists and played havoc with the mailing room generally. Just imagine the effects upon capitalism were the Appeal to have its millions of readers apply the same tactics!

Upon learning that "accidents" had happened to fifty thousand yards of cloth, during the trial of Ettor, Giovannitti and Caruso, William Wood is reported to have said "They are beating us at our own game." Surely no one can seriously claim that sabotage in the textile industry did not help to cement the various workers all the more closely together.

Even were it true that sabotage worked against solidarity to some extent, still it would have to receive consideration as an economic factor. It is sure to remain in use. It is co-existent with human slavery. **No analysis of the labor movement is complete where sabotage is not accepted as a weapon.**

Just as sabotage must differ in each industry so also must it change with industrial development. Should capitalism create an oligarchy to crush out all labor organization the attempt would be met by destructive sabotage. The degree of destruction would depend upon the measure of repression.

But should matters follow their present course, with the possibility of the workers gaining an ever increasing amount of industrial control, then labor's tactics will develop accordingly, with constructive sabotage as the result.

XI

To every positive there must be a negative and in all cases destruction must precede construction. Therefore, there is no absurdity in the term "constructive sabotage."

Sabotage may mean the direct destruction of property. Again it may mean indirect destruction through organized inefficiency. Or as an alterative it may proceed from a greater degree of efficiency than is desired by the employing class. This last is the point toward which sabotage tends when coupled with class solidarity.

The direct destruction of property for immediate individual benefit or to make a gain for a small group is but the following out of the theory of economic determinism. As such no revolutionist can condemn it. The indirect destruction of property for group benefit may also be a class weapon. It may be abused, but so may any other means of warfare. Like the strike, the fear of its use has as great a power as its direct application. The constructive qualities, in such a case, comes from its power to solidify labor. **A consciousness of economic might springs from the knowledge thus gained, that the employers have no force save that given by the labor of the slave class.**

As solidarity is produced there comes an added feeling of responsibility upon the organized workers. Gaining more and more the control of industry they realize that ere long the management of the whole of society will rest in their hands. Sabotage, which is sure to be used to long as a slave class exists, will then take on a definitely constructive character.

It is already the trend for sabotage to be directed more against the product than the machine. As the idea of an injury to one being an injury to all sinks in more thoroughly we shall see products sabotaged in a different manner—constructively.

The workers are coming to see that their class is the one to whom adulterated food, shoddy clothing and rotten materials are sold, and by refusing to adulterate products they not only destroy the employers' profits but safeguard their own lives as well. The bakers can gain the same result by putting the best of materials in the bread and pastry as they can by inserting coal oil. The secret refusal of packing house workers to handle rotten meats certainly is constructive from a class or a social viewpoint. Yet such actions are as fatal to the employers' profits as is the direct destruction of products. In fact it does mean the destruction of alum in bakeries, of "slunk" calves in packing houses, of "shoddy" in the woolen mills, and the destruction of capitalist property in profits.

The mass of workers are already propertyless. No tie binds them to our so-called civilization. Sabotage, for protection as well as for revenge, appeals to them. They have nothing to lose and much to gain by its use. Their economic condition calls for sabotage as a weapon against oppression. This mass must be impregnated with the ideal of working-class control of industry so their sabotage may take on a constructive character. That ideal is already firing the brains and nerving the hands of thousands of migratory workers.

Without apologizing for sabotage in any form, it can be said that constructive sabotage is destined to be a vital power in the class struggle from now until Capitalism falls and the industries are operated by the producers of all wealth.

XII

With the workers in full control of industry it is evident that all able bodied adults will be required to take part in the productive process. This means an end to classes and class rule; the disappearance of the political state; and the carrying on of production for use instead of for profit. Industrial brotherhood will have ended the terrible civil war in industry and sabotage will naturally cease when the reason for its existence is removed. In an Industrial Democracy, where the productivity of the whole body would be reflected in the life of the individual and the acts of the individual in turn would be a contribution to all of society, it is inconceivable that sabotage would still be carried on. Any continuation of its use over an extended period would show the necessity for another industrial adjustment to secure the real objects of the revolution.

Should the victory of the workers be forestalled by State Socialism, or governmental ownership of industry, it would be a signal for an increased use of sabotage on the part of the industrialists. The governmental tendency to regard a strike of state employees as treason to be curbed by court martial, would be met by a strike on the job through the medium of sabotage. Many of the present congressmen have already stated that they regard the formation of a labor union among postal employees as illegal and that a strike would mean nothing less than treason to the government. The postal employees need run no risk of being court martialed or even dismissed from the service. In mass sabotage they have a weapon which may be used in an entirely legal but none the less effective manner. They can obey all rules. The example was given by some

Austrian postal workers some two years ago, as reported in the Saturday Evening Post.

In order to gain certain demands, without losing their jobs, the Austrian postal workers strictly observed the rule that all mail matter must be weighed to see if the proper postage was affixed. Formerly they had passed, without weighing all those letters and parcels which were clearly under weight, thus living up to the spirit of the regulation but not to its exact wording. By taking each separate piece of mail matter to the scales, carefully weighing same and then returning it to its proper place, the postal workers had the office congested with unweighed mail on the second day. This method is more effective than striking, especially when used on a large scale.

In 1905 the railway workers of Italy gave a good example of the value of legal sabotage. They simply remained at their accustomed places and obeyed all the rules and regulations. When a person purchased a ticket they had to present the exact change. When they failed to comply, the rule in question was read to them. The wicket closed exactly on the set time, leaving long lines of waiting passengers. Inside the yards the same thing was going on. Every car was examined to make sure that it was in good condition. Every nut and bolt was tested before a car was allowed to leave the yard. Switching engines moved at the rate of speed called for in the regulations. When the indignant passengers tried to leave the cars they were held by the station guards and were shown the rule that forbade them to leave. Trains were thus held for hours, and finally when released from the station they were not allowed to run beyond the legal rate of speed and all signals were scrupulously observed. The service was completely demoralized within a short time.

So sabotage may be expected not only to form an increasingly popular weapon against capitalism, but also to be a means of bringing about the speedy downfall of any governmental ownership schemes that may be hatched for the purpose of blocking the road to industrial freedom. **Only with the gaining of industrial freedom will sabotage stop.**

XIII

When a strike breaks out the employers are quick to seize some prominent figures in the fight to place under arrest on serious charges. This in itself is not a bad thing for it has the immediate effect of solidifying the strikers. But when these arrests are multiplied to such an extent that special publicity cannot be had in each case, and conviction results, the workers are weakened. The increasing contempt for legal procedure will automatically shut off funds to support such cases unless it can be shown that the propaganda value of the trials is equal to the amount of cash expended. Yet it is certain that no organization proclaiming that, "An injury to one is an injury to all" can abandon any of the victimized workers. New tactics must be employed in such cases. **Sabotage is the most logical weapon to force a discontinuance of the practice of arresting strike leaders.**

Let the capitalist be reasonably certain that any attempt to judicially strangle the spokesmen of the workers will be met by a prolonged series of mishaps in the industries, and their hands will be stayed. Let the depriving of the workers of their liberty be a signal to deprive the employer of all profits, and arrests will cease to multiply. Law is a thing in which the wage slaves play no part, but industry, is the place where the employers are impotent when the workers decide to act. The same thing may be applied to cases where active union men, committee members, etc. are discharged. The employer generally starts his blacklist work at a season when a strike is undesirable from a working-class viewpoint, and the discharges may even be for the purpose of provoking a premature strike. Sabotage should be the answer to the disruptive attempts of the employers. Then again, there are minor grievances in the shops which the employer refuses to adjust and which are scarcely serious enough to warrant the tying up of industry. After due notification sabotage can be employed to gain the demands. This is especially true where the whole body are not class conscious enough to engage in an intermittent or irritation strike.

Sabotage has been called a confession of weakness because of its use when a strike has failed, where a strike is not advisable, and where the organization is without mass power because of being in the process of formation. Admitting the charge, is it not true that the workers are still largely without consciousness of power? It would be suicidal to act on the theory that we are today clothed with the might for which we are struggling. Being weak we must guard our embryonic organization, using every means within our grasp save that of compromise with our enemy, the employing class.

Another childish charge is that sabotage cannot gain any benefit for the workers that could not as well be gained by thorough industrial organization. Can the battles of the present be fought with the weapons of the future? We are not armed today with thorough organization, but **every toiler in the industries has sabotage at his command.** With thorough industrial organization there would be no wage system and it is idle to suppose that the capitalists will allow the workers to build a union to displace them without making strenuous attempts to wreck the structure. Sabotage can be used as a means of fighting capitalism in its attempts to stop the creating of a new society. The above mentioned argument sounds strangely like that of the socialist politician. We are told to elect a mayor to prevent violence against striking workers. Suggesting that the militia would be sent if the mayor refused to protect private property according to his oath of office we are told that the governor also must be elected before we strike. When the regular army is employed we are gravely informed that a socialist president is the necessary article to win strikes with. Then to crown it we are told by some that strikes will cease when a socialist is president, while others maintain that the president will abolish his office and turn the industries over to the workers.

But strike leaders are being jailed and active rebels victimized now and we must meet conditions as they exist and not as they will be when the present system is overthrown. Sabotage is a weapon of the existing daily combat between the masters and the slaves.

XIV

"Open Mouth" sabotage shows the weapon in its best form, a form which allows the spy but little place to act; which does not allow use of police; which strikes at the fraudulent practices on which Capitalism is based.

Commerce today is founded on fraud. Capitalism's standard of honesty demands that the wage slave lie to everyone except his employer. An honest business man is a myth and an honest clerk could not sell the shoddy goods of the merchants. There is not a single portion of the commerce of the entire world where exact truthfulness would not spell financial ruin under present conditions.

In the foodstuffs industry open mouth sabotage is peculiarly potent. Its use will at once enlist the support of a large portion of the public. It becomes one of the highest social acts. Let the workers, instead of striking, or even when on strike, expose the methods of manufacture and the boss will soon come to terms.

Let the workers in the candy factories tell of the glucose, terra alba and other poisonous substances in the candies and the consumer becomes hostile to the manufacturer.

Let the cooks tell how food is prepared for the table: of how foul meats are treated with chemicals so they may be served; let the dishwashers, waiters and other hotel and restaurant workers tell of conditions under which dishes are "washed" and the orders "prepared," and the employers will be forced into submission.

Let the building workers make known the substitution that invariably takes place in erecting structures by contract.

Let the firemen spread the news of boilers in which steam is generated to a dangerous point in order to save expenses.

The factory workers can tell of goods piled up beyond the fire limit. The workers engaged in the building of bridges, dams, reservoirs and structures of a similar nature, can tell of inferior materials used therein and of methods of construction not according to specifications, ofttimes being the direct cause of many deaths. Workers on the railroads can tell of faulty engines, unsafe trestles. Marine transport workers would do well to tell of the insufficient number of lifeboats, of inferior belts, and so forth. The textile worker can tell of the shoddy which is sold as "wool."

The persistent use of open mouth sabotage, besides gaining the demands of the workers, will be more effective in bringing about the stoppage of adulteration of foods than "pure foods laws" or other remedial legislation.

Nor does open mouth sabotage end there. The workers carry with them the secrets of the masters. Let them divulge these secrets, whether they be secret methods of manufacture that competitors are striving to learn, or acts of repression directed against the workers. **Let the masters know that henceforth they must deal with industrial mutiny.**

Both France and this country can record cases where it has been found expedient to have loyal workers pose as detectives so as to ferret out the secrets of the masters' guardians. The famous case in Boise, Idaho, is one example; and in nearly every great battle the working-class forces are forewarned of some of the intended attacks.

With this effectual, form of sabotage we do not think that even the reformer can quarrel. In fact, he is a party to it at all times and he justifies it on humanitarian grounds.

CONCLUSION
Labor produces all wealth—all wealth belongs to labor.

We, the workers, mental and manual, with our muscle, mind and skill, wrest raw materials from the breast of Nature and with infinite pain fashion them into the things of social value. We are the creators—to us belong the products. So far as actual productive processes are concerned we are in possession of industry, yet we have neither ownership nor control because of an absurd belief in property rights.

We stand aghast at the things of our own making. We create property and let it master us. We build thing great and small and we who are greater than all stand in abject fear of our own creations; foolishly thinking them to have some supernatural power—some force outside ourselves.

Property and precedent rule us all today and the precedents rest, one and all, upon a property basis. Things of flesh and blood and bone and sinew and tissue are held cheap as compared to the things of iron and steel and stone and brick and wood. "Property is robbery," said Proudhon. If this means that reverence for "property rights" is the basis of all exploitation, then Proudhon was right. The idea that wealth is greater than its creators has enslaved the world's toilers.

We have damned ourselves because we have thought that the right of the bakeshop and the bread was greater than the right of the working man's empty stomach. That same foolish belief has crowded countless thousands into death-dealing tenements, while on the healthy outskirts of the city there are numerous vacant dwellings. Garment workers are out at the elbows while the warehouse shelves groan, beneath their load of clothing. "Property" is indeed a hideous Frankenstein which will destroy us unless we are first able to destroy the sanctity with which it is surrounded.

Sabotage is discredited by those who believe in property rights. It is the weapon of those who no longer reverence the thing that fetters them. Its advocacy and use help to destroy the "property illusion." The parasites, who have property, oppose sabotage, while the producers, who have poverty, are commencing to wield that potent weapon.

Is the machine more than its makers? Sabotage says "No!"

Is the product greater than producers? Sabotage says "No!"

Sabotage places human life—and especially the life of the only useful class—higher than all else in the universe.

Will you keep private property and public poverty, master class morals and working-class misery, capitalism and crime—or will you arise in your outraged manhood and take a stand for sabotage, solidarity and a new social order in which there will be neither master nor slave? **For sabotage or for slavery? Which?**

—FINIS—

Glen Ellen, Sonoma Co., Cal.,

Dec. 5, 1913.

Dear Comrade Smith:—

Just a line to tell you that I have finished reading your pamphlet SABOTAGE. I do not find a point in it on which I disagree with you. It strikes me as a straight-from-the-shoulder, clear, convincing, revolutionary statement of the meaning and significance of sabotage.

Yours for the Revolution,

JACK LONDON.

We Are Coming Home, John Farmer—
We Are Coming Back to Stay

Cartoon by Ralph Chaplin for the IWW's
Agricultural Workers' Organization (1916)

Silent Agitator Sticker
by Ralph Chaplin (circa 1916)

SABOTAGE

Elizabeth Gurley Flynn

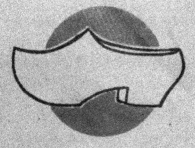

Ten Cents

I.W.W. Publishing Bureau
112 Hamilton Av.
CLEVELAND · OHIO

Sabotage

The Conscious Withdrawal of the Workers' Industrial Efficiency

Elizabeth Gurley Flynn

Sabotage

The Interest in sabotage in the United States has developed lately on account of the case of Frederic Sumner Boyd in the state of New Jersey, as an aftermath of the Paterson strike. Before his arrest and conviction for advocating sabotage, little or nothing was known of this particular form of labor tactic in the United States. Now there has developed a two-fold necessity to advocate it: not only to explain what it means to the worker in his fight for better conditions, but also to justify our fellow-worker Boyd in everything that he said. So I am desirous primarily to explain sabotage, to explain it in this two-fold significance, first as to its utility and second as to its legality.

Its Necessity in the Class War.

I am not going to attempt to justify sabotage on any moral ground. If the workers consider that sabotage is necessary, that in itself makes sabotage moral. Its necessity is its excuse for existence. And for us to discuss the morality of sabotage would be as absurd as to discuss the morality of the strike or the morality of the class struggle itself. In order to understand sabotage or to accept it at all it is necessary to accept the concept of the class struggle. If you believe that between the workers on the one side and their employers on the other there is peace, there is harmony such as exists between brothers, and that consequently whatever strikes and lockouts occur are simply family squabbles; if you believe that a point can be reached whereby the employer can get enough and the worker can get enough, a point of amicable adjustment of industrial warfare and economic distribution, then there is no justification and no explanation of sabotage intelligible to you. Sabotage is one weapon in the arsenal of labor to fight its side of the class struggle. Labor realizes, as it becomes more intelligent, that it must have power in order to accomplish anything; that neither appeals for sympathy nor abstract rights will make for better conditions. For instance, take an industrial establishment such as a silk mill where men and women and little children work ten hours a day for an average wage of between six and seven dollars a week. Could any one of them, or a committee representing the whole, hope to induce the employer to give better conditions by appealing to his sympathy, by telling him of the misery, the hardship and the poverty of their lives; or could they do it by appealing to his sense of justice? Suppose that an individual working man or woman went to an employer and said: "I make, in my capacity as wage worker in this factory, so many dollars worth of wealth every day and justice demands that you give me at least half." The employer would probably have him removed to the nearest lunatic asylum. He would consider him too dangerous a criminal to let loose on the community! It is neither sympathy nor justice that makes an appeal to the employer. But it is power. If a committee can go to the employer with this ultimatum: "We represent all the men and woman in this shop. They are organized in a union as you are organized in manufacturers' association. They have met and formulated in that union a demand for better hours and wages and they are not going to work one day longer unless they get it. In other words, they have withdrawn their power as wealth producers from your plant and they are going to coerce you by this withdrawal of their power; into granting their demands," that sort of ultimatum served upon an employer usually meets with an entirely different response: and, if the union is strongly enough organized and they are able to make good their threat they usually accomplish what tears and pleadings never could have accomplished.

We believe that the class struggle existing in society is expressed in the economic power of the master on the one side and the growing economic power of the workers on the other side meeting in open battle now and again, but meeting in continual daily conflict over which shall have the larger share of labor's product and the ultimate ownership of the means of life. The employer wants long hours, the intelligent workingman wants short hours. The employer wants low wages, the intelligent workingman wants high wages. The employer is not concerned with the sanitary conditions in the mill, he is concerned only with keeping the cost of production at a minimum; the intelligent workingman is concerned, cost or no cost, with having ventilation, sanitation and lighting that will be conducive to his physical welfare. Sabotage is to the class struggle what guerrilla warfare is to the battle. The strike is the open battle of the class struggle, sabotage is the guerilla warfare, the day-by-day warfare between two opposing classes.

General Forms of Sabotage.

Sabotage was adopted by the General Federation of Labor of France in 1897 as a recognized weapon in their method of conducting fights on their employers. But sabotage as an instinctive defense existed long before it was ever officially recognized by any labor organization. Sabotage means primarily: **the withdrawal of**

efficiency. Sabotage means either to slacken up and interfere with the quantity, or to botch in your skill and interfere with the quality, of capitalist production or to give poor service. Sabotage is not physical violence, sabotage is an internal, industrial process. It is something that is fought out within the four walls of the shop: And these three forms of sabotage to affect the quality, the quantity and the service are aimed at effecting the profit the employer. Sabotage is a means of striking at the employer's profit for the purpose of forcing him into granting certain conditions, even as workingmen strike for the same purpose of coercing him. It is simply another form of coercion.

There are many forms of interfering with efficiency, interfering with quality and the quantity of production: from varying motives there is the employer's sabotage as well as the worker's sabotage. Employers interfere with the quality of production, they interfere with the quantity of production, they interfere with the supply as well as with the kind of goods **for the purpose of increasing their profit.** But this form of sabotage, capitalist sabotage, is anti-social, for the reason that it is aimed at the good of the few at the expense of the many, whereas working-class sabotage is distinctly social, it is aimed at the benefit of the many, at the expense of the few.

Working-class sabotage is aimed directly at "the boss" and at his profits, in the belief that that is his religion, his sentiment, his patriotism. Everything is centered in his pocket book, and if you strike that you are striking at the most vulnerable point in his entire moral and economic system.

Short Pay, Less Work. "Ca Canny."

Sabotage as it aims at the quantity is a very old thing, called by the Scotch "Ca canny." All intelligent workers have tried it at some time or other when they have been compelled to work too hard and too long. The Scotch dockers had a strike in 1889 and their strike was lost, but when they went back to work they sent a circular to every docker in Scotland and in this circular they embodied their conclusions, their experience from the bitter defeat. It was to this effect. "The employers like the scabs, they have always praised their work, they have said how much superior they were to us, they have paid them twice as much as they have ever paid us: now let us go back on the docks determined that since those are the kind of workers they like and that is the kind of work they endorse we will do the same thing. We will let the kegs of wine go over the docks as the scabs did. We will have great boxes of fragile articles drop in the midst of the pier as the scabs did. We will do the work just as clumsily, as slowly, as destructively, as the scabs did. And we will see how long our employers can stand that kind of work." It was very few months until through this system of sabotage they had won everything they had fought for and not been able to win through the strike. This was the first open announcement of sabotage in an English-speaking country.

I have heard of my grandfather telling how an old fellow come to work on the railroad and the boss said, "Well, what can you do?"

"I can do most anything," said he—a big husky fellow.

"Well," said the boss, "can you handle a pick and shovel?"

"Oh, sure. How much do you pay on this job?"

"A dollar a day."

"Is that all? Well,—all right. I need the job pretty bad. I guess I will take it." So he took his pick and went leisurely to work. Soon the boss came along and said:

"Say, can't you work any faster than that?"

"Sure I can."

"Well, why don't you?"

"This is my dollar-a-day clip."

"Well," said the boss, "let's see what the $1.25-a-day clip looks like."

That went a little better. Then the boss said, "Let's see what the $1.50-a-day clip looks like." The man showed him. "That was fine," said the boss, "well, maybe we will call it $1.50 a day." The man volunteered the information that his $2-a-day clip was "a hummer" So, through this instinctive sort of sabotage this poor obscure workingman on a railroad in Maine was able to gain for himself an advance from $1 to $2 a day. We read of the gangs of Italian workingmen, when the boss cuts their pay—you know, usually they have an Irish or American boss and he likes to rake a couple of dollars a day on the side for himself, so he cuts the pay of the men once in a while without consulting the contractor and pockets the difference. One boss cut them 25 cents a day. The next day he came on the work, to find that the amount of dirt that was being removed had lessened considerably. He asked a few questions:

"What's the matter?"

"Me no understan' English"—none of them wished to talk.

Well, he exhausted the day going around trying to find one person who could speak and tell him what was wrong. Finally he found one man, who said, "Well you see, boss, you cutta da pay, we cutta da shob."

That was the same form of sabotage—to lessen the quantity of production in proportion to the amount of pay received. There was an Indian preacher who went to college and eked out an existence on the side by preaching. Somebody said to him, "John, how much do you get paid?"

"Oh, only get paid $200 a year."

"Well, that's damn poor pay, John."

"Well," he said, "Damn poor preach!"

That, too, is an illustration of the form of sabotage that I am now describing to you, the "ca canny" form of sabotage, the "go easy" slogan, the "slacken up, don't work so hard" species, and it is a reversal of the motto of the American Federation of Labor, that most "safe, sane and conservative" organization of labor in America. They believe in "a fair day's wage for a fair day's work." Sabotage is an unfair day's work for an unfair day's wage. It is an attempt on the part of the worker to limit his production in proportion to his remuneration. That is one form of sabotage.

Interfering with the Quality of Goods.

The second form of sabotage is to deliberately interfere with the quality the goods. And in this we learn many lessons from our employers, even as we learn how to limit the quantity. You know that every year in the western part of this United States there are fruits and grains produced that never find a market; bananas and oranges rot on the ground, whole skiffs of fruits are dumped into the ocean. Not because people do not need these foods and couldn't make good use of them in the big cities of the east, but because the employing class prefer to destroy a large percentage of the production in order to keep the price up in cities like New York, Chicago, Baltimore and Boston. If they sent all the bananas that they produce into the eastern part of the United States we would be buying bananas at probably three for a cent. But by destroying a large quantity, they are able to keep the price up to two for 5c. And this applies to potatoes, apples, and very many other staple articles required by the majority of people. Yet if the worker attempts to apply the same principle, the same theory, the same tactic as his employer we are confronted with all shorts of finespun moral objections.

Boyd's Advice to Silk Mill Slaves.

So it is with the quality. Take the case of Frederic Sumner Boyd, in which we should all be deeply interested because it is evident Frederic Sumner Boyd is to be made "the goat" by the authorities in New Jersey. That is to say, they want blood, they want one victim. If they can't get anybody else they are determined they are going to get Boyd, in order to serve a two-fold purpose to cow the workers of Paterson, as they believe they can, and to put this thing, sabotage, into the statutes, to make it an illegal thing to advocate or to practice. Boyd said this: "If you go back to work and you find scabs working alongside of you, you should put a little bit of vinegar on the reed of the loom in order to prevent its operation." They have arrested him under the statute forbidding the advocacy of the destruction of property. He advised the dyers to go into the dye houses and to use certain chemicals in the dyeing of the silk that would tend to make that silk unweavable. That sounded very terrible in the newspapers and very terrible in the court of law. But what neither the newspapers nor the courts of law have taken any cognizance of is that these chemicals **are being used already** in the dyeing of the silk. It is not a new thing that Boyd is advocating, it is something that is being practiced in every dye house in the city of Paterson already, but it is being practiced for the employer and not for the worker.

"Dynamiting" Silk.

Let me give you a specific illustration of what I mean. Seventy-five years ago when silk was woven into cloth the silk skein was taken in the pure, dyed and woven, and when that piece of silk was made it would last for 50 years. Your grandmother could wear it as a wedding dress. Your mother could wear it as a wedding dress. And then you, if you, woman reader, were fortunate enough to have a chance to get married, could wear it as a wedding dress also. But the silk that you buy today is not dyed in the pure and woven into a strong and durable product. One pound of silk goes into the dye house and usually as many as three to fifteen pounds come out. That is to say, along with the dyeing there is an extraneous and an unnecessary process of what is very picturesquely called "dynamiting." They weight the silk. They have solutions of tin, solutions of zinc, solutions of lead. If you will read the journals of the Silk Association of America you will find in there advice to master dyers as to which salts are the most appropriate for weighting purposes. You will read advertisements—possibly you saw it reprinted in "The Masses" for December, 1913—of silk mills, Ashley & Bailey's in Paterson, for instance, advertised by an auctioneer as having a plant for weighting, for dynamiting silk par excellence. And so when you buy a nice piece of silk today and have a dress made for festive occasions, you hang it away in the wardrobe and when you take it out it is cracked down the pleats and along the waist and arms. And you believe that you have been terribly cheated by a clerk. What is actually wrong is that you have paid for silk where you have received old tin cans and zinc and lead and things or that sort. You have a dress that is garnished with silk, seasoned with silk, but a dress that is adulterated to the point where, if it was adulterated just the slightest degree more it would fall to pieces entirely.

Now, what Frederic Sumner Boyd advocated to the silk workers was in effect this: "You do for yourselves what you are already doing for your employers. Put these same things into the silk for yourself and your own purposes as you are putting in for the employers, purposes." And I can't imagine—even in a court of law—where they can find the fine thread of deviation—where the master dyers' sabotage is legal and the worker's sabotage illegal, where they consist of identically the same thing and where the silk remains intact. The silk is there. The loom is there. There is no property destroyed by the process. The one thing that is eliminated is the efficiency of the worker to cover up this adulteration of the silk, to carry it just to the point where it will weave and not be detected. That efficiency is withdrawn. The veil is torn from off production in the silk-dyeing houses and silk mills and the worker simply says, "Here, I will take my hands off and I will show you what it is. I will show you how rotten, how absolutely unusable the silk actually is that they are passing off on the public at two and three dollars a yard."

Non-Adulteration and Over-Adulteration.

Now, Boyd's form of sabotage was not the most dangerous form of sabotage at that. If the judges had any imagination they would know that Boyd's form of sabotage was pretty mild compared with this: Suppose that he had said to the dyers in Paterson, to a sufficient number of them that they could do it as a whole, so that it would affect every dye house in Paterson: "Instead of introducing these chemicals for adulteration, don't introduce them at all. Take the lead, the zinc, and the tin and throw it down the sewer and weave the silk, beautiful, pure, durable silk just as it is. Dye it pound for pound, hundred pound for hundred pound." The employers would have been more hurt by that form of sabotage than by what Boyd advocated. And they would probably have wanted him put in jail for life instead of for seven years. In other words, to advocate non-adulteration is a lot more dangerous to capitalist interests than to advocate adulteration. And non-adulteration is the highest form of sabotage in an establishment like the dye house of Paterson, bakeries, confectioners, meat packing houses, restaurants, etc.

Interfering with quality, or durability, or the utility of a product, might be illustrated as follows: Suppose a milkman comes to your house every day and delivers a quart of milk and this quart of milk is half water and they put some chalk in it and some glue to thicken it. Then a milk driver goes on that round who belongs to a union. The union strikes. And they don't win any better conditions. Then they turn on the water faucet and they let it run so that the mixture is four-fifths water and one-fifth milk. You will send the "milk" back and make a complaint. At the same time that you are making that complaint and refusing to use the milk, hundreds and thousands of others will do the same thing, and through striking at the interests of the consumer once they are able to effect better conditions for themselves and also they are able to compel the employers to give the pure product. That form of sabotage is distinctly beneficial to the consumer. Any exposure of adulteration, any over-adulteration that makes the product unconsumable is a lot more beneficial to the consumer than to have it tinctured and doctored so that you can use it but so that it is destructive to your physical condition at the same time.

Interfering with quality can be instanced in the hotel and restaurant kitchens. I remember during the hotel workers strike they used to tell us about the great cauldrons of soup that stood there month in and month out without ever being cleaned, that were covered with verdigris and with various other forms of animal growth, and that very many times into this soup would fall a mouse or a rat and he would be fished out and thrown aside and the soup would be used just the same. Now, can anyone say that if the workers in those restaurants, as a means of striking at their employers, would take half a pound of salt and throw it into that soup cauldron, you as a diner, or consumer, wouldn't be a lot better off? It would be far better to have that soup made unfit for consumption than to have it left in a state where it can be consumed but where it is continually poisonous to a greater or less degree. Destroying the utility of the goons sometimes means a distinct benefit to the person who might otherwise use the goods.

Interfering with Service. "Open Mouth" Sabotage.

But that form of sabotage is not the final form of sabotage. Service can be destroyed as well as quality. And this accomplished in Europe by what is known as "the open mouth sabotage." In the hotel and restaurant industry, for instance—I wonder if this judge who sentenced Boyd to seven years in state's prison would believe in this form of sabotage or not? Suppose he went into a restaurant and ordered a lobster salad and he said to the spick and span waiter standing behind the chair, "Is the lobster salad good?" "Oh, yes, sir," said the waiter. "It is the very best in the city." That would be acting the good wage slave and looking out for the employer's interest. But if the waiter should say, "No, sir, it's rotten lobster salad. It's made from the pieces that have been gathered together here for the last six weeks," that would be the waiter who believed in sabotage, that would be the waiter who had no interest in his boss' profits, the waiter who didn't give a continental whether the boss sold lobster salad or not. And the judge would probably believe in sabotage in that particular instance. The waiters in the city of New York were only about 5,000 strong. Of these, about a thousand were militant, were the kind that could be depended on in a strike. And yet that little strike made more sensation in New York City than 200,000 garment workers who were out at the same time. They didn't win very much for themselves, because of their small numbers, but they did win a good deal in demonstrating their power to the employer to hurt his business. For instance, they drew up affidavits and they told about every hotel and restaurant in New York, the kitchen and the pantry conditions. They told about how the butter on the little butter plates was sent back to the kitchen and somebody with their fingers picked out cigar ashes and the cigarette butts and the matches and threw the butter back into the general supply. They told how the napkins that had been on the table, used possibly by a man who had consumption or syphilis, were used to wipe the dishes in the pantry. They told stories that would make your stomach sick and your hair almost turn white, of conditions in the Waldorf, the Astor, the Belmont, all the great restaurants and hotels in New York. And I found that that was one of the most effective ways of reaching the public, because the "dear public" are never reached through sympathy. I was taken by a lady up to a West Side aristocratic club of women who had nothing else to do, so they organized this club. You know—the white-gloved aristocracy! And I was asked to talk about the hotel workers' strike. I knew that wasn't what they wanted at all. They just wanted to look at what kind of person a "labor agitator" was. But I saw a chance for publicity for the strikers. I told them about the long hours in the hot kitchens; about steaming, smoking ranges. I told them about the overwork and the underpay of the waiters and how these waiters had to depend upon the generosity or the drunkenness of some patron to give them a big tip; all that sort of thing. And they were stony-faced. It affected them as much as an arrow would Gibraltar. And then I started to tell them about what the waiters and the cooks had told me of the kitchen conditions and I saw a look of frozen horror on their faces immediately. They were interested when I began to talk about something that affected their own stomach, where I never could have reached them through any appeal for humanitarian purposes. Immediately they began to draw up resolutions and to cancel engagements at these big hotels and decided that their clubs must not meet there again. They caused quite a commotion around some of the big hotels in New York. When the workers went back to work after learning that this was a way of getting at the boss via the public stomach they did not hesitate at sabotage in the kitchens. If any of you have ever got soup that was not fit to eat, that was too salty or peppery, maybe shorter hours, and that was one way they notified there where some boys in the kitchen that wanted the boss. In the Hotel McAlpin the head waiter called the men up before him after the strike was over and lost and said, "Boys, you can have what you want, we will give you the hours, we will give you the wages, we will give you everything, but, for God's sake, stop this sabotage business in the kitchen!" In other words, what they had not been able to win through the strike they were able to win by striking at the taste of the public, by making the food non-consumable and therefore compelling the boss to take cognizance of their efficiency and their power in the kitchen.

Following the "Book of Rules."

Interfering with service may be done in another way. It may be done, strange to say, sometimes by abiding by the rules, living up to the law absolutely. Sometimes the law is almost as inconvenient a thing for the capitalist as for a labor agitator. For instance, on every railroad they have a book of rules, a nice little book that they give to every employee, and in that book of rules it tells how the engineer and the fireman must examine every part of the engine before they take it out of the round house. It tells how the brakeman should go the length and the width of the train and examine every bit of machinery to be sure it's in good shape. It tells how the station master should do this and the telegraph operator that, and so forth, and it all sounds very nice in the little book. But now take the book of rules and compare it with the timetable and you will realize how absolutely impossible the whole thing is. What is it written for? An accident happens. An engineer who has been working 36 hours does not see a signal on the track, and many people are killed. The coroner's jury meets to fix the responsibility. And upon whom is it fixed? This poor engineer who didn't abide by the book of rules! He is the man upon whom the responsibility falls. The company wipe their hands and say, "We are not responsible. Our employee was negligent. Here are our rules." And through this book of rules they are able to fix the responsibility of every accident on some poor devil like that engineer who said the other day, after a frightful accident, when he was arrested, "Yes, but if I didn't get the train in at a certain time I might have lost my job under the new management on the New Haven road." That book of rules exists in Europe as well. In one station in France there was an accident and the station master was organized in the Railwaymen's Union. And they went to the union and asked for some action. The union said, "The best thing for you men to do is to go back on the job and obey that book of rules letter for letter. If that is the only reason why accidents happen we will have no accidents hereafter." So they went back and when a man came up to the ticket office and asked for a ticket to such and such a place, the charge being so much and would hand in more than the amount he would be told, "Can't give you any change. It says in the book of rules a passenger must have the exact fare." This was the first one. Well, after a lot of fuss they chased around and got the exact change, were given their tickets and got aboard the train. Then when the train was supposedly ready to start the engineer climbed down, the fireman followed and they began to examine every bolt and piece of mechanism on the engine. The brakeman got off and began to examine every thing he was supposed to examine. The passengers grew very restless. The train stood there about an hour and a half. They proceeded to leave the train. They were met at the door by an employee who said, "No, it's against the rules for you to leave the train once you get into it, until you arrive at your destination." And within three days the railroad system of France was so completely demoralized that they had to exonerate this particular station master, and the absurdity of the book of rules had been so demonstrated to the public that they had to make over their system of operation before the public would trust themselves to the railroads any further.

This book of rules has been tried not only for the purpose of exoneration: it has been tried for the purpose of strikes. Where men fail in the open battle they go back and with this system they win. Railroad men can sabotage for others as well as for themselves. In a case like the miners of Colorado where we read there that militiamen were sent in against the miners. We know that they are sent against the miners because the first act of the militia was to disarm the miners and leave the mine guards, the thugs, in possession of their arms. Ludlow followed! The good judge O'Brien went into Calumet, Mich., and said to the miners—and the president of the union, Mr. Moyer, sits at the table as chairman while he said it—"Boys, give up your guns. It is better for you to be shot than it is to shoot anybody." Now, sabotage is not violence, but that does not mean that I am deprecating all forms of violence. I believe for instance in the case of Michigan, in the case of Colorado, in the case of Roosevelt, N.J., the miners should have held onto their guns, exercised their "constitutional right" to bear arms, and, militia or no militia, absolutely refused to give them up until they saw the guns of the thugs and the guns of the mine guards on the other side of the road first. And even then it might be a good precaution to hold on them in case of danger! Well, when this militia was being sent from Denver up into the mining district one little train crew did what has never been done in America before; something that caused a thrill to go through the humblest toiler. If I could have worked for twenty years just to see one little torch of hope like that, I believe it worthwhile. The train was full of soldiers. The engineer, the fireman, all the train crew stepped out of the train and they said, "We are not going to run this train to carry any soldiers in against our brother strikers." So they deserted the train, but it was then operated by a

Baldwin detective and a deputy sheriff. Can you say that wasn't a case where sabotage was absolutely necessary?

Putting the Machine on Strike.

Suppose that when the engineer, had gone on strike he had taken a vital part of the engine on strike with him, without which it would have been impossible for anyone to run that engine. Then there might have been a different story. Railroad men have a mighty power in refusing to transport soldiers, strike-breakers and ammunition for soldiers and strike-breakers into strike districts. They did in Italy. The soldiers went on the train. The train guards refused to run the trains. The soldiers thought they could run the train themselves. They started, and the first signal they came to was "Danger." They went along very slowly and cautiously, and the next signal was at "Danger." And they found before they had gone very far that some of the switches had been turned and they were run off on to a siding in the woods somewhere. Laboriously they got back onto the main track. They came to a drawbridge and the bridge was turned open. They had to go across in boats and abandon the train. That meant walking the rest of the way. By the time they got into the strike district the strike was over. Soldiers who hare had to walk aren't so full of vim and vigor and so anxious to shoot "dagoes" down when they get into a strike district as when they ride in a train manned by union men.

The railroad men have mighty power in refusing to run these trains and putting them in such a condition that they can't be run by others. However, to anticipate a question that is going to be asked about the possible disregard for human life remember that when they put all the signals at danger there is very little risk for human life, because the train usually has to stop dead still.

Where they take a vital part of the engine away the train does not run at all. So human life is not in danger. They make it a practice to strike such a vital blow that the service is paralyzed thereafter.

With freight of course they do different things. In the strike of the railroad workers in France they transported the freight in such a way that a great trainload of fine fresh fruit could be run off into a siding in one of the poorest districts of France. It was left decay. But it never reached the point of either decay or destruction. It was usually taken care of by the poor people of that district. Something that was supposed to be sent in a rush from Paris to Havre was sent to Marseilles. And so within a every short time the whole system was so clogged and demoralized that they had to say to the railroad workers, "You are the only efficient ones. Come back. Take your demands. But run our railroads."

"Print the Truth or You Don't Print at All."

Now, what is true of the railroad workers is also true of the newspaper workers. Of course one can hardly imagine any more conservative element to deal with than the railroad workers and the newspaper workers. Sometimes you will read a story in the paper that is so palpably false, a story about strikers that planted dynamite in Lawrence for instance (and it came out in a Boston paper before the dynamite was found), a story of how the Erie trains were "dynamited" by strikers in Paterson; but do you realize that the man who writes that story, the man who pays for that story, the owners and editors are not the ones that put the story into actual print? It is put in print by printers, compositors, typesetters, men who belong to the working class and are members of unions. During the Swedish general strike these workers who belonged to the unions and were operating the papers rebelled against printing lies against their fellow strikers. They sent an ultimatum to the newspaper managers: "Either you print the truth or you'll print no papers at all." The newspaper owners decided they would rather print no paper at all than tell the truth. Most of them would probably so decide in this country, too. The men went on strike and the paper came out, a little bit of sheet, two by four, until eventually they realized that the printers had them by the throat that they could not print any papers without the printers. They sent for them to come back and told them "So much of the paper will belong to the strikers and they can print what they please in it."

But other printers have accomplished the same results by the sabotage. In Copenhagen once there was a peace conference and a circus going on at the same time. The printers asked for more wages and they didn't get them. They were very sore. Bitterness in the heart is a very good stimulus for sabotage. So they said, "All right, we will stay right at work boys, but we will do some funny business with this paper so they won't want to print it tomorrow under the same circumstances." They took the peace conference where some high and mighty person was going to make an address on international peace and they put that man's speech in the circus news; they reported the lion and the monkey as a making speeches in the peace conference and the Honorable Mr. So-and-so doing trapeze acts in the circus. There was great consternation and indignation in the city. Advertisers, the peace conference, the circus protested. The circus would not pay their bill for advertising. It cost the paper as much, eventually, as the increased wages would have cost them, so that they came to the men figuratively on their bended knees and asked them, "Please be good and we will give you whatever you ask." That is the power of interfering with industrial efficiency by a competent worker.

"Used Sabotage, But Didn't Know What You Called It."

Sabotage is for the workingman an absolute necessity. Therefore it is almost useless to argue about its effectiveness. When men do a thing instinctively continually, year after year and generation after generation, it means that that weapon has some value to them. When the Boyd speech was made in Paterson, immediately some of the socialists rushed to the newspapers to protest. They called the attention of the authorities to the fact that the speech was made. The secretary of the socialist party and the organizer of the socialist party repudiated Boyd. That precipitated the discussion into the strike committee as to whether speeches on sabotage were to be permitted. We had tried to instill into the strikers the idea that any kind of speech was to be permitted; that a socialist or a minister or a priest; an IWW man, an anarchist, anybody should have the platform. And we tried to make the strikers realize. "You have sufficient intelligence to select for yourselves. If you haven't got that, then no censorship over your meetings is going to do you any good." So they had a rather tolerant spirit and they were not inclined to accept this socialist denunciation of sabotage right off the reel. They had an executive session and threshed it out and this is what occurred.

One worker said, "I never heard of this thing called sabotage before Mr. Boyd spoke about it on the platform. I know once in a while when I want a half-day off and they won't give it to me I slip the belt off the machine so it won't run and I get my half-day. I don't know whether you call that sabotage, but that's what I do."

Another said, "I was in the strike of the dyers eleven years ago and we lost. We went back to work and we had these scabs that had broken our strike working side by side with us. We were pretty sore. So whenever they were supposed to be mixing green we saw to it that they put in red, or when they were supposed to be mixing blue we saw to it that they put in green. And soon they realized that scabbing was a very unprofitable business. And the next strike we had, they lined up with us. I don't know whether you call that sabotage, but it works."

As we went down the line, one member of, the executive committee after another admitted they had used this, thing but they "didn't know that was what you called it!" And so in the end democrats, republicans, socialists, all IWW's in the committee voted that speeches on sabotage were to be permitted, because it was ridiculous not to say on the platform what they were already doing in the shop.

And so my final justification of sabotage is its constant use by the worker. The position of speakers, organizers, lecturers, writers who are presume to be interested in the labor movement, must be one of two. If you place yourself in a position outside of the working class and you presume to dictate to them from some "superior" intellectual plane, what they are to do, they will very soon get rid of you, for you will very soon demonstrate that you are of absolutely no use to them. I believe the mission of the intelligent propagandist is this: we are to see what the workers are doing, and then try to understand why they do it; not tell them it's right or it's wrong, but analyze the condition and see if possibly they do not best understand their need and if, out of the condition, there may develop a theory that will be of general utility. Industrial unionism, sabotage are theories born of such facts and experiences. But for us to place ourselves in a position of censorship is to alienate ourselves entirely from sympathy and utility with the very people we are supposed to serve.

Sabotage and "Moral Fiber."

Sabotage is objected to on the ground that it destroys the moral fiber of the individual, whatever that is! The moral fiber of the workingman! Here is a poor workingman, works twelve hours a day seven days a week for two dollars a day in the steel mills of Pittsburg. For that man to use sabotage is going to destroy his moral fiber. Well, if it does, then moral fiber is the only thing he has left. In a stage of society where men produce a completed article, for instance if a shoemaker takes a piece of raw leather, cuts it, designs it, plans the shoes makes every part of the shoes, turns out a finished product, that represents to him what the piece of sculpturing represents to the artist, there is joy in handicraftsmanship, there is joy in labor. But can anyone believe that a shoe factory worker, one of a hundred men, each doing a small part of the complete whole, standing before a machine for instance and listening to this ticktack all day long—that such a man has any joy in his work or any pride in the ultimate product? The silk worker for instance may make beautiful things, fine shimmering silk. When it is hung up in the window of Altman's or Macy's or Wanamaker's it looks beautiful. But the silk worker never gets a chance to use a single yard of it. And the producing of the beautiful thing instead of being a pleasure is instead a constant aggravation to the silk worker. They make a beautiful thing in the shop and then they come home to poverty, misery, and hardship. They wear a cotton dress while they are weaving the beautiful silk for some demi monde in New York to wear.

I remember one night we had a meeting of 5,000 kiddies. (We had them there to discuss whether or not there should be a school strike. The teachers were not telling the truth about the strike and we decided that the children were either to hear the truth or it was better for them not to go to school at all.) I said, "Children, is there any of you here who have a silk dress in your family? Anybody's mother got a silk dress?" One little ragged urchin in front piped up. "Shure, me mudder's got a silk dress."

I said, "Where did she get it?"—perhaps a rather indelicate question, but a natural one.

He said, "Me fadder spoiled the cloth and had to bring home."

The only time they get a silk dress is when they spoil the goods so that nobody else will use it: when the dress is so ruined that nobody else would want it. Then they can have it. The silk worker takes pride in his product! To talk to these people about being proud of their work is just as silly as to talk to the street cleaner about being proud of his work, or to tell the man that scrapes out the sewer to be proud of his work. If they made an article completely or if they made it all together under a democratic association and then they had the disposition of the silk—they could wear some of it, they could make some of the beautiful salmon-colored and the delicate blues into a dress for themselves—there would be pleasure in producing silk. But until you eliminate wage slavery and the exploitation of labor it is ridiculous to talk about destroying the moral fiber of the individual by telling him to destroy "his own product." Destroy his own product! He is destroying somebody else's enjoyment, somebody else's chance to use his product created in slavery. There is another argument to the effect that "If you use this thing called sabotage you are going to develop in yourself a spirit of hostility, a spirit of antagonism to everybody else in society, you are going to become sneaking, you are going to become cowardly. It is an underhanded thing to do." But the individual who uses sabotage is not benefiting himself alone. If he were looking out for himself only he would never use sabotage. It would be much easier, much safer not to do it. When a man uses sabotage he is usually intending to benefit the whole; doing an individual thing but doing it for the benefit of himself and others together. And it requires courage. It requires individuality. It creates in that workingman some self-respect for and self-reliance upon himself as a producer. I contend that sabotage instead of being sneaking and cowardly is a courageous thing, is an open thing. The boss may not be notified about it through the papers, but he finds out about it very quickly, just the same. And the man or woman who employs it is demonstrating a courage that you may measure in this way: How many of the critics would do it? How many of you, if you were dependent on a job in a silk town like Paterson, would take your job in your hands and employ sabotage? If you were a machinist in a locomotive shop and had a good job, how many of you would risk it to employ sabotage? Consider that and, then you have the right to call the man who uses it a coward—if you can.

Limiting the Over-Supply of Slaves.

It is my hope that workers will not only "sabotage" the supply of products, but also the over-supply of producers. In Europe the syndicalists have carried on a propaganda that we are too cowardly to carry on in the United States as yet. It is against the law. Everything is "against the law," once it becomes large enough for the law to take cognizance that it is in the best interests of the working class. If sabotage is to be thrown aside because it is construed as against the law, how do we know that next year free speech may not have to be thrown aside? Or free assembly or free press? That a thing is against the law, does not mean necessarily that the thing is not good. Sometimes it means just the contrary: a mighty good thing for the working class to use against the capitalists. In Europe they are carrying on this sort of limitation of product: they are saying, "Not only will we limit the product in the factory, but we are going to limit the supply of producers. We are going to limit the supply of workers on the market." Men and women of the working class in France and Italy and even Germany today are saying, "We are not going to have ten, twelve and fourteen children for the army, the navy, the factory and the mine. We are going to have fewer children, with quality and not quantity accentuated as our ideal who can be better fed, better clothed, better equipped mentally and will become better fighters for the social revolution." Although it is not a strictly scientific definition I like to include this as indicative of the spirit that produces sabotage. It certainly is one of the most vital forms of class warfare there are, to strike at the roots of the capitalists system by limiting their supply of slaves on their own behalf.

Sabotage a War Measure.

I have not given you a rigidly defined thesis on sabotage because sabotage is in the process of making. Sabotage itself is not clearly defined. Sabotage is as broad and changing as industry, as flexible as the imagination and passions of humanity. Every day workingmen and women are discovering new forms of sabotage, and the stronger their rebellious imagination is the more sabotage they are going to invent, the more sabotage they are going to develop. Sabotage is not however, a permanent weapon. Sabotage is not going to be necessary, once a free society has been established. Sabotage is simply a war measure and it will go out of existence with the war, just as the strike, the lockout, the policeman, the machine gun, the judge with his injunction, and all the various weapons in the arsenals of capital and labor will go out of existence with the advent of a free society. "And then," someone may ask, "may not this instinct for sabotage have developed, too far, so that one body of workers will use sabotage against another; that the railroad workers, for instance, will refuse to work for the miners unless they get exorbitant returns for labor?" The difference is this: when you sabotage an employer you are saboting somebody upon whom you are not interdependent, you have no relationship with him as a member of society contributing to your wants in return for your contribution. The employer is somebody who depends absolutely on the workers. Whereas, the miner is one unit in a society where somebody else supplies the bread, somebody else the clothes, somebody else the shoes, and where he gives his product in exchange for someone else's; and it would be suicidal for him to assume a tyrannical, a monopolistic position, of demanding so much for his product that the others might cut him off from any other social relations and refuse to meet with any such bargain. In other words, the miner, the railroad worker, the baker is limited in using sabotage against his fellow workers because he is interdependent on his fellow workers, whereas he is not materially interdependent on the employer for the means of subsistence.

But the worker will not be swerved from his stern purpose by puerile objections. To him this is not an argument but a struggle for life. He knows freedom will come only when his class is willing and courageous enough to fight for it. He knows the risk, far better than we do. But his choice is between starvation in slavery and starvation in battle. Like a spent swimmer in the sea, who can sink easily and apathetically into eternal sleep, but who struggles on to grasp a stray spar, suffers but hopes in suffering—so the worker makes his choice. His wife's worries and tears spur him forth to don his shining armor of industrial power; his child's starry eyes mirror the light of the ideal to him and strengthen his determination to strike the shackles from the wrists of toil before that child enters the arena of industrial life; his manhood demands some rebellion against daily humiliation and intolerable exploitation.

To this worker, sabotage is a shining sword. It pierces the nerve centers of capitalism, stabs at its hearts and stomachs, tears at the vitals of its economic system. It is cutting a path to freedom, to ease in production and ease in consumption.

Confident in his powers, he hurls his challenge into his master's teeth—I am, I was and I will be—

"I will be, and lead the nations on, the last of all
	your hosts to meet,
Till on your necks, your heads, your crowns, I'll
	plant my strong, resistless feet.
Avenger, Liberator, Judge, red battles on my
	pathway hurled,
I stretch forth my almighty arm till it revivifies
	the world."

PUBLISHER'S NOTE.

The reference to the case of Frederick Sumner Boyd, which is found in several places in the text of the foregoing pamphlet, requires additional explanation. The pamphlet was written more than two years ago, since which time some interesting developments have occurred in Boyd's case. After being convicted on the charge of "advising the destruction of property" Boyd carried his case to the New Jersey Court of Errors and Appeals, where the lower court was sustained. Boyd was then taken into custody, and sent to the state prison in Trenton a sentence of "from two to seven years." He immediately signed a petition for pardon in which he professes to have repudiated his former ideas, and to have renounced the advocacy of sabotage an all other subversive ideas. In view of Boyd's apparent cowardice in the presence of the pamphlet is about to go to press, we add this note for the sake of clearness.

About the Editor and Authors

Salvatore Salerno is the author of *Red November, Black November: Culture and Community in the Industrial Workers of the World* and has contributed articles to the *Haymarket Scrapbook* and many other publications. He is a professor on the Community Faculty staff of Metropolitan State University in St. Paul, Minnesota.

William Ernst Trautmann (1869–1940) was a leading theorist and founding general secretary-treasurer of the Industrial Workers of the World (IWW) and one of six people who initially laid plans for the organization in 1904. Between 1905 and 1912 he mostly worked in the field as an organizer. In 1922 Trautmann published a novel, *Riot*, that drew on his experiences as an IWW activist during the Pressed Steel Car Strike of 1909 in McKees Rocks, Pennsylvania.

Walker C. Smith (1885–1927) was a leading member of the IWW, who wrote and edited socialist newspapers, philosophical tracts, pamphlets, satirical plays, and even verse. Smith regularly went on speaking tours to promote the cause of the Wobblies and recruit new members. Since Smith was a "noted IWW agitator," police arrested him frequently for his union activities. Smith's most famous pamphlet, *Sabotage*, was used by courts throughout the United States as evidence that members of the IWW union were guilty of criminal syndicalism for simply belonging to the union. Though *Sabotage* was probably Smith's most widely distributed pamphlet, his most famous work was *The Everett Massacre*, a book intended to reveal the injustices committed against the working classes of Everett, Washington.

Elizabeth Gurley Flynn, "The Rebel Girl" (1890–1964) was a labor leader, activist, and feminist who played a leading role in the IWW. Flynn was a founding member of the American Civil Liberties Union and a visible proponent of women's rights, birth control, and women's suffrage.

About
PM Press

PM Press was founded at the end of 2007 by a small collection of folks with decades of publishing, media, and organizing experience. PM Press co-conspirators have published and distributed hundreds of books, pamphlets, CDs, and DVDs. Members of PM have founded enduring book fairs, spearheaded victorious tenant organizing campaigns, and worked closely with bookstores, academic conferences, and even rock bands to deliver political and challenging ideas to all walks of life. We're old enough to know what we're doing and young enough to know what's at stake.

We seek to create radical and stimulating fiction and nonfiction books, pamphlets, T-shirts, visual and audio materials to entertain, educate, and inspire you. We aim to distribute these through every available channel with every available technology, whether that means you are seeing anarchist classics at our bookfair stalls; reading our latest vegan cookbook at the café; downloading geeky fiction e-books; or digging new music and timely videos from our website.

Contact us for direct ordering and questions about all PM Press releases, as well as manuscript submissions, review copy requests, foreign rights sales, author interviews, to book an author for an event, and to have PM Press attend your bookfair:

PM Press • PO Box 23912 • Oakland, CA 94623
510-658-3906 • info@pmpress.org

Buy books and stay on top of what we are doing at:

www.pmpress.org

FOPM

MONTHLY SUBSCRIPTION PROGRAM

These are indisputably momentous times—the financial system is melting down globally and the Empire is stumbling. Now more than ever there is a vital need for radical ideas.

In the six years since its founding—and on a mere shoestring—PM Press has risen to the formidable challenge of publishing and distributing knowledge and entertainment for the struggles ahead. With over 250 releases to date, we have published an impressive and stimulating array of literature, art, music, politics, and culture. Using every available medium, we've succeeded in connecting those hungry for ideas and information to those putting them into practice.

Friends of PM allows you to directly help impact, amplify, and revitalize the discourse and actions of radical writers, filmmakers, and artists. It provides us with a stable foundation from which we can build upon our early successes and provides a much-needed subsidy for the materials that can't necessarily pay their own way. You can help make that happen—and receive every new title automatically delivered to your door once a month—by joining as a Friend of PM Press. And, we'll throw in a free T-shirt when you sign up.

Here are your options:

- $30 a month: Get all books and pamphlets plus 50% discount on all webstore purchases
- $40 a month: Get all PM Press releases (including CDs and DVDs) plus 50% discount on all webstore purchases
- $100 a month: Superstar—Everything plus PM merchandise, free downloads, and 50% discount on all webstore purchases

For those who can't afford $35 or more a month, we're introducing *Sustainer Rates* at $15, $10 and $5. Sustainers get a free PM Press T-shirt and a 50% discount on all purchases from our website.

Your Visa or Mastercard will be billed once a month, until you tell us to stop. Or until our efforts succeed in bringing the revolution around. Or the financial meltdown of Capital makes plastic redundant. Whichever comes first.

REBEL VOICES
An IWW Anthology

Edited by Joyce L. Kornbluh
Preface by Daniel Gross
Contributions by Franklin Rosemont
Introduction by Fred Thompson
$27.95 • 472 Pages • 10 by 7
ISBN: 978-1-60486-483-0

Welcoming women, Blacks, and immigrants long before most other unions, the Wobblies from the start were labor's outstanding pioneers and innovators, unionizing hundreds of thousands of workers previously regarded as "unorganizable." Wobblies organized the first sit-down strike (at General Electric, Schenectady, 1906), the first major auto strike (6,000 Studebaker workers, Detroit, 1911), the first strike to shut down all three coalfields in Colorado (1927), and the first "no-fare" transit-workers' job-action (Cleveland, 1944). With their imaginative, colorful, and world-famous strikes and free-speech fights, the IWW wrote many of the brightest pages in the annals of working class emancipation.

Wobblies also made immense and invaluable contributions to workers' culture. All but a few of America's most popular labor songs are Wobbly songs. IWW cartoons have long been recognized as labor's finest and funniest.

The impact of the IWW has reverberated far beyond the ranks of organized labor. An important influence on the 1960s New Left, the Wobbly theory and practice of direct action, solidarity, and "class-war" humor have inspired several generations of civil rights and antiwar activists, and are a major source of ideas and inspiration for today's radicals. Indeed, virtually every movement seeking to "make this planet a good place to live" (to quote an old Wobbly slogan), has drawn on the IWW's incomparable experience.

Originally published in 1964 and long out of print, *Rebel Voices* remains by far the biggest and best source on IWW history, fiction, songs, art, and lore. This new edition includes 40 pages of additional material from the 1998 Charles H. Kerr edition from Fred Thompson and Franklin Rosemont, and a new preface by Wobbly organizer Daniel Gross.

Socialist and Labor Songs
An International Revolutionary Songbook

Edited by Elizabeth Morgan
Preface by Utah Phillips
$14.95 • 96 Pages • 11 by 8.5
ISBN: 978-1-60486-392-5

Seventy-seven songs—with words and sheet music—of solidarity, revolt, humor, and revolution. Compiled from several generations in America, and from around the world, they were originally written in English, Danish, French, German, Italian, Spanish, Russian, and Yiddish.

From IWW anthems such as "The Preacher and the Slave" to Lenin's favorite 1905 revolutionary anthem "Whirlwinds of Danger," many works by the world's greatest radical songwriters are anthologized herein: Edith Berkowitz, Bertolt Brecht, Ralph Chaplin, James Connolly, Havelock Ellis, Emily Fine, Arturo Giovannitti, Joe Hill, Langston Hughes, William Morris, James Oppenheim, Teresina Rowell, Anna Garlin Spencer, Maurice Sugar—and dozens more.

Old favorites and hidden gems, to once again energize and accompany picket lines, demonstrations, meetings, sit-ins, marches, and May Day parades.

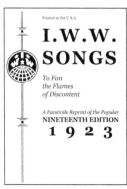

I.W.W. Songs

$5.95 • 64 pages • 5.5x4
ISBN: 978-1-60486-950-7

Undoubtedly the most popular book in American labor history, the I.W.W.'s *Little Red Song Book* has been a staple item on picket lines and at other workers' gatherings for generations, and has gone through numerous editions.

The steadily mounting interest in Wobbly history and culture warrants this facsimile edition of a classic *Little Red Song Book* from the union's Golden Age. Reprinted here is the Nineteenth Edition, originally issued in 1923, the year the I.W.W. reached its peak membership.

Ninety years ago these songs were sung with gusto in Wobbly halls and hobo jungles from Brooklyn to San Pedro. And they're still fun to sing today!